NEW YORK
Cult Recipes

MARC GROSSMAN

NEW YORK
Cult Recipes

Photographs
AKIKO IDA AND PIERRE JAVELLE

Illustrations of New York
JANE TEASDALE

STERLING EPICURE
New York

THE CULT RECIPES OF A NEW YORKER

My grandparents emigrated to New York from Russia. I went in the opposite direction and consequently have spent the last 13 years as a New Yorker in Paris. People are always asking me if I miss New York and seem shocked that I chose to leave. The truth is I like being a New Yorker in Paris more than being a New Yorker in New York, where, let's face it, we're a dime a dozen. It's kind of like Superman. On earth, he's a superhero—*faster than a speeding bullet … able to leap tall buildings in a single bound.* But back on Krypton (with its presumably higher gravitational pull), he'd just be one Kryptonian among others, a mere pedestrian going about his not-particularly heroic business. Not to suggest that New Yorkers are some sort of super race, or that living there is a bore, but being an expat does have its perks. For starters, you get to actually miss and appreciate all those things you once took for granted. And if you're like me, this phenomenon will manifest itself almost exclusively through food. What begins as a minor homesick craving—say, for a fresh bialy from Kossar's or a piece of cheesecake from Junior's—builds into a full-blown culinary obsession. The next thing you know you've spent two weeks trying to make the perfect fill-in-the-blank from your composite food memories, which pretty much explains this book. Basically, these are the recipes I crave most when I miss New York and, as such, they reflect my own idiosyncratic experience of New York food—a mix of Greek diners, Jewish delis, old-school Chinatown, American junk food, American health food, and a bunch of other stuff tossed into the melting pot. Put it all together and you've got a one-way ticket to NYC. Enjoy the flight! **M.G.**

7 : 10

COFFEE TIME

FILTERED COFFEE

Unlimited refills of filtered coffee is a longstanding tradition in New York diners. We call it a bottomless cup, and this is surely one of the reasons why New York is called "the city that never sleeps." In recent years, the once-humble cup of filtered coffee has been gaining in prestige as a new wave of coffee afficionados work on preparing it with scientific precision using freshly ground coffee beans. My friend Thomas Lehoux, one of the founders of the Parisian coffee club, Frog Fight, and co-owner of Café Réné, was one of the first to promote this style of coffee in Paris. Here are his instructions for making a perfect cup at home.

MAKES 1 CUP

Preparation time: 5 minutes

WHAT YOU NEED

a kettle
a dripper (preferably Hario®)
a coffee pot
a filter (preferably Kalita®)
freshly roasted whole coffee beans
a set of scales
a coffee grinder

Step 1. Boil some water in the kettle.

Step 2. Put the dripper on the coffee pot and the filter into the dripper. When the water boils, pour a little into the filter to rinse it out and remove the paper taste. Warm the coffee pot as well.

Step 3. Weigh out the coffee. The general rule is: 2¼ oz coffee to 4 cups water. So for 1¾ cups water, I use 1 oz coffee. Grind the coffee to filter coffee size—you should be able to feel the particles between your fingers. It looks like a powder to the eye.

Step 4. Measure out 1¾ cups water. Put the coffee in the middle of the filter and add ⅓ cup of the water. Wait for 30 seconds (to de-gas the coffee), then slowly add the remaining water. It should take about 2½ minutes for all the water to filter through to your coffee pot (if this is not the case, grind the coffee more finely and increase the volume of water). Don't stir the coffee grinds with a spoon, let the water flow through by itself.

Step 5. Enjoy your coffee.

ICED COFFEE

Use the same method, adding ice to the jug after rinsing the filter, and reduce the equivalent weight of the ice from the water.

CHALLAH

This braided loaf, traditionally eaten for Shabbat, is New York's answer to the French brioche.

MAKES 1 LOAF

Preparation time: 45 minutes, plus cooling
Resting time: 2½ hours
Cooking time: 25 minutes

DRY INGREDIENTS

3¾ cups cake flour
1½ teaspoons dried yeast
¼ cup superfine sugar
2 teaspoons fine salt

WET INGREDIENTS

⅔ cup lukewarm water
2 eggs
2 egg yolks
2 tablespoons olive oil

GLAZE

1 tablespoon egg white
1 teaspoon superfine sugar

THE DOUGH

Combine the dry ingredients, then beat together the wet ingredients. Carefully combine the two mixtures and knead until the dough is very elastic (5–10 minutes in a machine, 10–20 minutes by hand). Form a smooth ball of dough, place it in an oiled container and cover with plastic wrap. Let it rise at room temperature for about 1½ hours until it has doubled in volume.

SHAPING THE DOUGH

Divide the dough into six equal portions. Using the palms of your hands, shape each portion into evenly shaped sausages about 12 inches long. On a baking sheet that's floured or lined with parchment paper, braid the sausages using the illustration as a guide. Sprinkle the braid lightly with flour, then cover loosely with plastic wrap. Let it rise at room temperature for at least 1 hour until it has doubled in volume.

COOKING

Preheat the oven to 350°F. Combine the egg white and sugar and brush it over the braid. Bake for about 25 minutes until the bread is golden brown. Allow to cool.

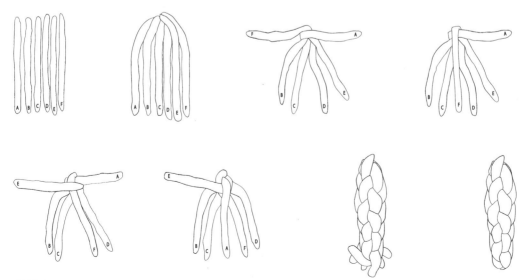

GREEN SMOOTHIE

In New York, Melvin's Juice Box is the place to go for green smoothies. In Paris, it's Bob's Juice Bar, and it's J.-P., the manager, who makes them.

SERVES 2

Preparation time: 5 minutes

INGREDIENTS

1 ripe banana, peeled and frozen

1 cup mineral water

1 huge handful baby spinach

1 tablespoon fresh herbs (mint or parsley)

3½ oz frozen mango flesh

Place everything in a blender, ending with the mango so you can adjust the quantity to make up 2 cups, and blend. If your blender isn't powerful enough to handle rock-hard frozen fruit, let the mixture soften for a few minutes before blending.

DOUGHNUTS

There's nothing like a fresh doughnut, like the ones you can get at Doughnut Plant on Manhattan's Lower East Side. Depending on where you live, you might have no choice but to make your own. You'll be glad you did.

MAKES ABOUT 20 DOUGHNUTS

Preparation time: 25 minutes, plus cooling
Resting time: 5½ hours
Cooking time: 2 minutes per doughnut

DOUGH

2½ oz coconut oil or
    sweet/unsalted butter, melted
1½ cups milk
5⅔ cups cake flour
3 teaspoons dried yeast
½ cup superfine sugar
2 eggs
1 egg yolk
1½ teaspoons natural vanilla extract
1½ teaspoons fine salt

FRYING

4 cups oil for frying* (or more depending
    on the size of the pot)

*Check the label on the oil. It
should specifically indicate that the
oil is appropriate for frying.

THE DOUGH

Combine the coconut oil or butter with the milk. Combine the flour with the yeast and sugar. Mix the eggs with the yolk, vanilla, and salt. Combine the three mixtures together. Knead until the dough is very elastic (5–10 minutes in a machine, 10–20 minutes by hand). Form a smooth ball of dough, place it in a greased container and cover with plastic wrap. Let it rise at room temperature for about 1½ hours until it has doubled in volume, then refrigerate for at least 3 hours.

SHAPING THE DOUGH

Roll out the dough on a floured surface. Use a cookie cutter to cut out perfectly circular or rectangular shapes. Using a large cookie cutter and a small one for the center will produce the classic wheel shape of a doughnut. For filled doughnuts (see page 24), the larger circle without a hole cut out is traditional.

The dough scraps can be gathered up into a new ball, rerolled, and recut one time. To avoid a second lot of scraps, I like to make regular shapes using a pastry cutter, leaving little-to-no excess dough between cuts, or I use the pastry cutter from the get-go to avoid scraps all together. It depends how important the look of the doughnuts is to you. Place each shape on an individual piece of parchment paper (otherwise it is difficult to pick up the doughnuts without damaging them when it comes time to fry). Sprinkle flour over the doughnuts to prevent them from sticking together, cover loosely with plastic wrap, and allow them to rise at room temperature for about 1 hour until they have doubled in volume again.

THE FRYING

Heat the oil in a pot until it reaches 350°F or until a cube of bread dropped into the oil turns golden brown in 15 seconds. Using the pieces of parchment paper to move the doughnuts, drop two or more at a time into the hot oil. Cook for about 2 minutes on each side until golden. Let the oil reheat for about 30 seconds between batches. Place the hot doughnuts on a wire rack or paper towels to drain excess oil. Allow to cool before glazing (see page 22).

DOUGHNUTS: GLAZES

**EACH GLAZE IS ENOUGH FOR
ABOUT 6 DOUGHNUTS**

HONEY

1 cup confectioners' sugar, sifted
1 teaspoon light honey
3 tablespoons sweet/unsalted butter,
    melted
1½ tablespoons hot water
½ teaspoon natural vanilla extract

VANILLA (WHITE)

1½ cups confectioners' sugar, sifted
1½ tablespoons milk
½ teaspoon natural vanilla extract
Add the milk gradually as you mix.
Add more milk if it's too thick to
dip, but the idea is for the frosting
to be as thick as possible so that
it will be opaque when it sets.

MAPLE SYRUP

1⅓ cups confectioners' sugar, sifted
3 tablespoons maple syrup
1 pinch salt

CHOCOLATE

2 tablespoons sweet/unsalted butter,
    melted
1½ oz chocolate, melted
½ cup confectioners' sugar, sifted
2 teaspoons hot water
The butter and chocolate can be
melted together over low heat in
a saucepan or double boiler.

THE GLAZING

For each glaze, simply mix all of the ingredients together in a bowl
with a spoon or fork until combined. Then, holding the doughnuts
in one hand, dip them in the glaze, turning them over the bowl to
allow the excess to drip back into the bowl before placing the
doughnuts on a wire rack to set. A little hot water can be added
to any of the glazes if they have become too thick. If topping with
chopped nuts, do so before the glaze sets to make sure they stick.

DOUGHNUTS: FILLINGS

Doughnuts are often filled with either jam or jelly and dusted with confectioners' sugar—Jelly Doughnuts—or filled with custard and topped with a chocolate glaze—Boston Creams.

FOR 1 DOUGHNUT

1½ tablespoons filling
1 piping/icing bag

THE TECHNIQUE FOR FILLING A DOUGHNUT

Place the filling (about 1½ tablespoons per doughnut) into a piping/icing bag fitted with a plain narrow piping nozzle. Poke a hole in your doughnut using a chopstick or something similar. Insert the nozzle into the hole and gently squeeze the filling into the doughnut. The doughnut will puff up and, when full, the filling will start oozing back out of the hole. In addition to jelly or jam, vanilla custard makes a great doughnut filling.

VANILLA CUSTARD

FOR 12 DOUGHNUTS

Preparation time: 15 minutes
Cooking time: 15 minutes

INGREDIENTS

3 teaspoons cornstarch
3 tablespoons sugar
1 pinch salt
1 cup milk
2 egg yolks
2 tablespoons sweet/unsalted butter
½ vanilla bean, split lengthways
    and seeds scraped out

THE MIXTURE

Make a slurry with the cornstarch, sugar, salt, and about 1 tablespoon of the milk. Mix the egg yolks with the rest of the milk. Combine the two mixtures in a saucepan.

COOKING

Heat over medium heat, whisking constantly. At the first sign of bubbles, remove from the heat but continue to whisk. When the custard starts to get smooth and thick, almost like a mayonnaise, stir in the butter and the scraped vanilla bean and seeds. If the custard needs more cooking to thicken, return the saucepan to a medium heat and stir constantly until thickened. Tip the custard into a bowl and cover with plastic wrap touching the surface of the custard to keep a skin from forming.

LEMON POPPY SEED MUFFINS

Of all the muffins we make at Bob's Juice Bar, this is my personal favorite.
J.-P. has been tweaking the recipe for years and they are truly irresistible.

MAKES 12 MUFFINS

Preparation time: 15 minutes, plus cooling
Cooking time: about 25 minutes

DRY INGREDIENTS

2¼ cups all-purpose flour
2 tablespoons + 1 teaspoon poppy seeds
½ teaspoon salt
3 teaspoons baking powder

WET INGREDIENTS

zest of 1 lemon, finely shredded
⅔ cup superfine sugar
½ cup sweet/unsalted butter, melted
2 eggs
3 tablespoons lemon juice
1 cup yogurt

FRUIT

3½ oz apple, shredded
3½ oz pear, seeded and diced

GLAZE

1 cup confectioners' sugar
1½ tablespoons lemon juice
3 teaspoons hot water

THE BATTER

Preheat the oven to 375°F. Combine all the dry ingredients together. Beat together the wet ingredients. Combine the two mixtures and fold in the fruit.

COOKING

Spoon the batter into a greased 12-hole muffin pan and bake for about 25 minutes until the muffins are golden brown, and a skewer inserted into the middle comes out clean. Cool.

THE GLAZING

Mix all of the glaze ingredients in a bowl until combined. Add more water if necessary or if you like a thinner glaze. For a thick white glaze like you see in the photo, don't add too much water—you want to add just enough water for the glaze to be liquid enough to dip the muffins into it.Plunge the head of each muffin into the mixture, allow the excess to drip back into the bowl, then place the muffins on a rack, top side up, and allow the glaze to set.

MANGO LASSI

See recipe page 28.

MANGO LASSI

MAKES 2 LASSIS

Preparation time: 5 minutes

INGREDIENTS

1 lb mango flesh
1 cup yogurt
3½ oz ice cubes
1–2 tablespoons honey
seeds of 2 cardamom pods

Set aside 3½ oz mango cut into pieces.
Blend all the rest of the ingredients together.
Pour into glasses and add the mango pieces.

BANANA BREAD

A classic cake in the form of a loaf. I like it moist with visible bits of banana and big chunks of chocolate.

MAKES ONE 9 X 5 INCH LOAF

Preparation time: 20 minutes, plus cooling
Cooking time: 55 minutes

DRY INGREDIENTS

1 cup + 1 tablespoon all-purpose flour
⅓ cup buckwheat flour
1½ teaspoons baking powder
1 teaspoon ground cinnamon

WET INGREDIENTS

⅓ cup light brown sugar
5 tablespoons sunflower oil
2 eggs
¾ cup sour cream
1 teaspoon natural vanilla extract

FILLINGS

5¾ oz banana (1 medium banana), finely
    diced or mashed with a fork
¾ cup dark chocolate, chopped into
    small pieces

THE BATTER

Preheat the oven to 350°F. Butter and flour a 9 × 5 inch loaf pan.
Combine the dry ingredients and beat together the wet ingredients. Stir the banana into the wet mixture and the chocolate into the dry mixture.
Combine the two mixtures without overworking the batter.

COOKING

Fill the pan three-quarters full with the batter. Bake for 45 minutes. Cover with foil and bake for a further 10 minutes. Allow to cool before serving.

note: To make a muffin version of the banana bread, spoon the batter into muffin pans, place a round of banana on top and bake for about 25 minutes at 350°F. This quantity of mixture makes about 10 muffins.

If you would like to glaze the banana bread as we have done, simply use the glaze recipe on page 26.

STREET FOOD

A huge street food scene which, from the hot dog seller in Central Park to the traditional shaved-ice snow cones on the west side of Brooklyn, reflects a hectic pace of life, an unbridled spirit of enterprise and, more than anything, an insatiable appetite.

BABKA

*This breakfast cake, which looks like a marbled brioche,
is a classic of New York's Jewish bakeries.*

MAKES 1 BABKA

Preparation time: 25 minutes
Resting time: 2½ hours
Cooking time: about 45 minutes

STREUSEL

⅓ cup cake flour
¼ cup sugar
2 tablespoons sweet/unsalted butter,
    softened
1 teaspoon ground cinnamon
1 oz dark/semi-sweet chocolate chips

DRY INGREDIENTS

2 cups cake flour
¾ teaspoon dried yeast
2 pinches salt
¼ cup superfine sugar

WET INGREDIENTS

6 tablespoons lukewarm buttermilk
1 egg
1 egg yolk
½ cup sweet/unsalted butter, melted
1 egg white, lightly whisked

FILLING

⅓ cup cocoa powder
½ cup + 1 tablespoon superfine sugar
2 teaspoons vanilla sugar
⅓ cup sweet/unsalted butter, softened

THE STREUSEL

Make the streusel by mixing all the ingredients together by hand
until crumbly. Set aside in the refrigerator for at least 30 minutes.

THE DOUGH

Combine the dry ingredients and beat together the wet ingredients,
except the egg white. Combine the two mixtures together. Knead
until the dough is very elastic (5–10 minutes in an electric mixer,
10–20 minutes by hand).
Form a smooth ball of dough, place it in an oiled container and
cover with plastic wrap. Let it rise at room temperature for about
1½ hours until it has doubled in volume.

THE FILLING

Combine the cocoa powder and sugars and set aside.

SHAPING THE DOUGH

On a floured work surface, roll out the dough into a rectangular
shape approximately 16 inches long. Spread over the softened butter
and sprinkle with the cocoa–sugar mixture. Roll the dough up along
its length. Bring the two ends together and twist three times. Butter
and flour a 8¼ × 3½ inch bar/loaf pan and place the dough twist
inside. Cover loosely with plastic wrap and allow it to rise at room
temperature for 1 hour until the dough is well risen.

COOKING

Preheat the oven to 350°F. Brush the surface of the babka with the
egg white and scatter over the streusel. Bake for about 45 minutes
until golden brown.

COFFEE CAKES

MAKES 14 CAKES

Preparation time: 20 minutes
Refrigeration time: 30 minutes
Cooking time: 35 minutes

STREUSEL

2 cups all-purpose flour
1⅔ cups light brown sugar
1 cup sweet/unsalted butter, softened
3 teaspoons ground cinnamon

WET INGREDIENTS

½ cup sweet/unsalted butter, softened
1 cup superfine sugar
1 teaspoon natural vanilla extract
2 eggs
⅔ cup buttermilk

DRY INGREDIENTS

2 cups all-purpose flour
2 teaspoons baking powder
2 pinches salt

INGREDIENTS

7¾ oz pear, seeded and thinly sliced

THE STREUSEL

Make the streusel by mixing all the ingredients together by hand
until crumbly. Set aside in the refrigerator for at least 30 minutes.

THE MIXTURE

Preheat the oven to 350°F. Beat the butter and sugar vigorously
until light and creamy. Mix in the rest of the wet ingredients.
Combine the dry ingredients and add to the wet mixture without
overworking the batter.

ASSEMBLY AND COOKING

Pour the batter to a depth of ½ inch into 14 buttered and floured
round 4½ inch cake pans. Add a few pear slices and top with the
streusel just out of the refrigerator (so the streusel holds together
better during cooking), without packing it down too much.
Bake for 30–35 minutes until a skewer inserted comes out clean.

CINNAMON ROLLS

To fully appreciate these cinnamon rolls, you should eat them just out of the oven, still dripping with cream cheese frosting.

MAKES 10 ROLLS

Preparation time: 30 minutes
Resting time: 2½ hours
Cooking time: about 12 or
    25 minutes (depending
    on the pan)

DOUGH

2⅔ cups all-purpose flour
1 teaspoon dried yeast
3 tablespoons lukewarm water
¼ cup lukewarm milk
3½ tablespoons sweet/unsalted
    butter, melted
1 egg
2 pinches salt
3 tablespoons superfine sugar
½ teaspoon natural vanilla extract

FILLING

⅓ cup sweet/unsalted butter,
    softened
¼ cup superfine sugar
4½ teaspoons ground cinnamon
1 tablespoon milk

FROSTING

¾ cup confectioners' sugar
3½ oz plain cream cheese, softened
2 tablespoons hot water

THE DOUGH

Combine the ingredients for the dough in a mixing bowl, then knead vigorously for 10–15 minutes. Place the dough in an oiled bowl, cover with plastic wrap and let it rest at room temperature for about 1½ hours until the dough has doubled in size.

SHAPING THE DOUGH

On a floured work surface, roll out the dough into a rectangle. Spread over the softened butter and sprinkle with the combined sugar and cinnamon. Roll the dough up along its length if you want to bake the rolls in a large pan, or widthways if you want to bake in individual pans. Cut 10 rolls and place them on a baking sheet lined with parchment paper or in individual well-buttered pans. Brush with the milk. Cover them loosely with plastic wrap, or a clean dish towel, and let them rise for 1 hour at room temperature until the dough is well risen.

COOKING

Preheat the oven to 400°F and bake the rolls until they're golden brown (allow about 12 minutes for individual rolls and about 25 minutes for a large pan). When they come out of the oven, mix the frosting ingredients together and spread over the rolls while still hot, with a spatula or brush. Serve hot if possible.

PECAN ROLLS

This is an upside-down variation of the cinnamon rolls.
These rolls contain pecans and are baked with a caramel topping.

MAKES 10 ROLLS

Preparation time: 30 minutes
Resting time: 2½ hours
Cooking time: about 15 minutes
    + 10 minutes for the pecans

DOUGH

2⅔ cups all-purpose flour
1 teaspoon dried yeast
3 tablespoons lukewarm water
¼ cup lukewarm milk
3½ tablespoons sweet/unsalted
    butter, melted
1 egg
2 pinches salt
3 tablespoons superfine sugar
½ teaspoon natural vanilla extract

TOPPING

2 cups pecans
¾ cup lightly packed light brown
    sugar (or ⅔ cup superfine sugar
    + 2 teaspoons molasses)
1½ tablespoons maple syrup
¼ cup sweet/unsalted butter, melted

FILLING

½ cup sweet/unsalted butter,
    softened
¼ cup superfine sugar
½ teaspoon natural vanilla extract

THE DOUGH

Combine the ingredients for the dough in a mixing bowl, then knead vigorously for 10–15 minutes. Place the dough in an oiled bowl, cover with plastic wrap, and let it rest at room temperature about 1½ hours until the dough has doubled in size.

THE TOPPING

Preheat the oven to 350°F. Spread the pecans on a baking sheet lined with parchment paper and bake for 10 minutes to lightly toast them. Allow to cool.

Butter and flour an 11¼ × 7½ inch pan. Mix the sugar, maple syrup, and melted butter by whisking together until combined, and place the pecans and this mixture in the base of the pan.

SHAPING THE DOUGH

On a floured work surface, roll out the dough into a rectangle. Spread over the softened butter, and sprinkle with the combined sugar and vanilla. Roll the dough up along its length. Cut 10 rolls and place them on top of the pecan caramel in the pan. Cover loosely with plastic wrap or a clean dish towel, and let rise at room temperature for 1 hour until the dough is well risen.

COOKING

Preheat the oven to 400°F, bake the rolls for about 15 minutes until they are golden brown. Turn them out onto a serving dish; the still-hot caramel will be flowing. Serve hot or lukewarm.

8 : 14

BREAKFAST TIME

BUTTERMILK FLAPJACKS

Classic flapjacks made with buttermilk.

MAKES 7 FLAPJACKS

Preparation time: 10 minutes
Cooking time: 3–5 minutes per flapjack

DRY INGREDIENTS

1¼ cups all-purpose flour
2 pinches baking soda
2 teaspoons baking powder
3 teaspoons superfine sugar
½ teaspoon salt

WET INGREDIENTS

1 cup buttermilk
2 eggs
5 tablespoons sweet/unsalted butter,
    melted
4 drops natural vanilla extract

OTHER INGREDIENTS

blueberries or other fruit (optional)
maple syrup and butter, to serve

THE BATTER

Combine the dry ingredients, beat together the wet ingredients, and whisk them into the dry mixture without overworking the batter. The batter should remain lumpy; if you mix until the batter is perfectly smooth, the flapjacks may turn out too tough.

COOKING

Heat a frying pan over medium heat with a little oil. I prefer coconut oil, but sunflower oil works as well. Test the frying pan with a small spoonful of batter: If it doesn't sizzle, the pan's not hot enough; if the bottom is too brown before bubbles appear on top, it's too hot. Adjust the heat so that the underside is golden when the top bubbles, but isn't dry yet.
Pour in a ladle for each flapjack and sprinkle with a few blueberries or other fruit if desired. When the underside is golden brown, flip the flapjack using a spatula and cook the other side for about 30–40 seconds. Serve hot with maple syrup and butter.

SILVER DOLLAR FLAPJACKS

Their name comes from the size of a one-dollar coin. Just as with money, you can never have too many of these super-light flapjacks.

MAKES 25 MINI FLAPJACKS

Preparation time: 10 minutes
Cooking time: 3–5 minutes per flapjack

DRY INGREDIENTS

1 cup all-purpose flour
1 teaspoon baking powder
1 teaspoon superfine sugar
1 pinch salt

WET INGREDIENTS

1 cup milk
2 eggs
5 teaspoons sweet/unsalted butter,
    melted
2 drops natural vanilla extract

OTHER INGREDIENTS

maple syrup and butter, to serve

THE BATTER

Combine the dry ingredients, beat together the wet ingredients, and whisk them into the dry mixture without overworking the batter. The batter should remain lumpy; if you mix until the batter is perfectly smooth, the flapjacks may turn out too tough.

COOKING

Heat a frying pan over medium heat with a little oil. I prefer coconut oil, but sunflower oil works as well. Test the frying pan with a small spoonful of batter: If it doesn't sizzle, the pan's not hot enough; if the bottom is too brown before bubbles appear on top, it's too hot. Adjust the heat so that the underside is golden when the top bubbles, but isn't dry yet.
Pour in 1 tablespoon for each mini flapjack. When the underside is golden brown, flip the flapjack using a spatula and cook the other side for about 30 seconds.
Serve hot with maple syrup and butter.

CANDIED BACON

See recipe page 88.

CHOCOLATE PROTEIN DRINK

One of J.-P.'s classics at Bob's Juice Bar, this is what I drink to reward myself after a session at the pool.

SERVES 2

Preparation time: 5 minutes

INGREDIENTS

2 bananas, peeled and frozen
1 measure of protein powder
1½ tablespoons cocoa powder
3 teaspoons maple syrup, agave syrup, or honey
1 cup mineral water

Combine all the ingredients together in a blender. You can also use fresh bananas instead of frozen and replace some of the mineral water with ice cubes.

BUCKWHEAT FLAPJACKS

*My mother likes to start her day with buckwheat flapjacks
at Big Nick's Greek diner. This is my dairy-free recipe.*

MAKES 8 FLAPJACKS

Preparation time: 20 minutes
Cooking time: 3–5 minutes per flapjack

DRY INGREDIENTS

1 cup buckwheat flour
1 cup all-purpose flour
2 teaspoons baking powder
3 teaspoons superfine sugar
½ teaspoon salt
2 pinches ground cinnamon

WET INGREDIENTS

2 drops natural vanilla extract
1 egg
6 tablespoons sunflower oil
1½ cups water
3 teaspoons baby oat flakes (cooked
   in ¼ cup water*) or quick oats

OTHER INGREDIENTS

sliced bananas or berries (optional) plus
   extra, to serve
maple syrup and butter, to serve

* Cook the baby oat flakes with the
water in a saucepan over medium heat
for about 5 minutes until the water is
absorbed. Remove from the heat and let
stand for a few minutes until the oats
come away from the base of the pan.

THE BATTER

Combine the dry ingredients, beat together the wet ingredients,
and whisk them into the dry mixture without overworking the
batter. The batter should remain lumpy; if you mix until the batter
is perfectly smooth, the flapjacks may turn out too tough.

COOKING

Heat a frying pan over medium heat with a little oil. I prefer
coconut oil, but sunflower oil works as well. Test the frying
pan with a small spoonful of batter: If it doesn't sizzle, the pan's
not hot enough; if the bottom is too brown before bubbles
appear on top, it's too hot. Adjust the heat so that the underside
is perfectly golden when the top bubbles, but isn't dry yet.
Pour in a ladle for each flapjack and sprinkle with berries
or a few slices of banana, if using. When the underside
is golden brown, flip the flapjack using a spatula and cook
the other side for about 30–40 seconds.
Serve hot with maple syrup, butter, and extra fresh fruit.

CHOCOLATE PROTEIN DRINK

See recipe page 48.

PEANUT BUTTER SMOOTHIE

*Like the peanut butter and
jelly sandwich, this smoothie
combines the flavors of berries
and peanut butter.*

SERVES 2
Preparation time: 5 minutes

INGREDIENTS
1 banana, peeled and frozen
4½ oz strawberries, washed, hulled, and frozen
2 dried medjool dates, pitted
2 tablespoons peanut butter (page 263)
1 cup* whatever milk you like (almond, rice,
   cow's, etc.)

* Or enough to make up a total volume
of 2 cups combined ingredients.

Blend all the ingredients together until you have
a creamy mixture. You can also use fresh fruit
instead of frozen and replace some of the water
with ice cubes.

COCONUT GRANOLA & DRIED MANGO

Eugénie, who helped me make the recipes in this book, makes the best granola I've ever tasted. No exaggeration. This recipe is especially addictive. It's the perfect topping for oatmeal, an acai cup (see page 256), yogurt, ice cream …

MAKES 1 SMALL BAKING SHEET OF GRANOLA

Preparation time: 20 minutes, plus cooling
Cooking time: 2 hours 45 minutes

DRIED MANGO

1 mango, ripe but not soft

DRY INGREDIENTS

1¼ oz Brazil nuts, roughly chopped
1¼ oz cashew nuts, roughly chopped
2 cups large rolled oats
1¼ oz unhulled sesame seeds
1½ oz shredded coconut
¼ cup sunflower seeds
¼ cup rice flour
¼ teaspoon salt

INGREDIENTS TO HEAT

5 tablespoons coconut oil or sunflower oil
1 tablespoon light brown sugar
5½ oz honey
1 teaspoon natural vanilla extract

DRIED MANGO

Preheat the oven to 200°F. Cut the mango into slices about ¼ inch thick and lay them flat on a baking sheet lined with parchment paper, making sure they don't overlap or touch. Place in the oven for about 45 minutes. Turn them over, then continue baking for a further 45 minutes. Allow them to cool, and then lay them flat in an airtight container between layers of parchment paper so they don't stick together.

THE GRANOLA

Preheat the oven to 300°F. Combine all the dry ingredients in a bowl.
In a large saucepan, heat the coconut oil, sugar, honey, and vanilla over medium heat, whisking constantly. Remove from the heat when the mixture starts to boil. Immediately pour over the dry ingredients and mix together carefully with a spatula. When the mixture is evenly coated, pour it onto a baking sheet lined with parchment paper, and spread out into a layer about ⅝ inch thick.

COOKING AND SERVING

Bake for about 40 minutes, checking its progress at regular intervals. If the granola is browning too quickly, reduce the oven temperature to 275°F, and cover the granola with a sheet of foil. When it starts to dry out and form clumps, remove the sheet from the oven and stir gently with a spatula. Return to the oven for 20–30 minutes. Cut up the mango slices if you need to and mix them into the granola, then return to the oven for 10 minutes. Allow to cool at room temperature before breaking the granola into pieces. The granola will keep for at least 3 weeks in an airtight container at room temperature.

note: You can store the dried mangoes for 1 month in an airtight container away from heat and moisture. They will stay soft and retain a melt-in-the-mouth texture.

tip: Depending on your taste, you can add shaved, dried coconut and fresh banana slices when serving.

HOT OATMEAL

A healthy alternative when you're looking for a comforting hot breakfast treat.

SERVES 2

Preparation time: 10 minutes
Cooking time: 5 minutes

INGREDIENTS

1¼ cups baby oat flakes
 or quick oats
2–2½ cups milk or water
½ teaspoon salt
3 teaspoons light brown sugar,
 honey, or agave syrup (optional)
½ teaspoon ground cinnamon or
 natural vanilla extract
2 teaspoons butter or peanut butter

PREPARATION

Combine all the ingredients, except the butter or peanut butter, in a saucepan, and cook over medium heat, stirring. After about 5 minutes, when it is good and thick, turn off the heat, add the butter or peanut butter, and let it sit for about 1 minute so that the oatmeal can set and come away from the base of the pan.

SERVING

Serve hot with fresh fruit, granola, the warm milk of your choice (cow's, soy, almond, etc.), seeds, and the sweetener of your choice (light brown sugar, maple syrup, honey, etc.).

PEANUT BUTTER SMOOTHIE

See recipe page 52.

BAGEL

See recipe page 72.

UPPER WEST SIDE

Located in the northwest of Manhattan, this neighborhood is a paradise for food lovers, with Greek restaurants like Tom's Restaurant, the Broadway Restaurant, and Big Nick's, kosher delis like Barney Greengrass and Murray's Sturgeon Shop, and two of New York's best markets: Fairway and Zabar's.

DINER

FILET OF MATJES HERRING
3 19 EA

MURRAY'S
FILET OF PICKLED HERRING IN CLEAR
3.49 EA.

MURRAY'S
FILET OF SCHMALTZ HERRING
3.99 EA.

SANDWICHES
BEEFBURGER 5.05
Onion · Cole Slaw · Pickle
BEEFBURGER DeLuxe 6.65
French Fries · Lettuce · Tomato
Cole Slaw · Pickle
CHEESEBURGER 5.45
Onion · Cole Slaw · Pickle
CHEESEBURGER DeLuxe 7.10
French Fries · Lettuce · Tomato
Cole Slaw · Pickle
BACON BURGER 5.65
BACON BURGER DeLuxe 7.25
French Fries · Lettuce · Tomato
Cole Slaw · Pickle
BACON CHEESEBURGER 6.05
BACON CHEESEBURGER DeLuxe 7.65
French Fries · Lettuce · Tomato
Cole Slaw · Pickle

2 EGGS Any Style 6.35
with 2 EGGS Potatoes & Toast
2 EGGS Any Style
BACON, HAM OR SAUSAGE
POTATOES & TOAST
1 EGG ANY STYLE with
BACON, HAM or SAUSAGE
CORNED BEEF HASH
with 1 EGG POTATOES & TOAST
PANCAKES with Syrup & Butter
with BACON, HAM or SAUSAGE
FRENCH TOAST Syrup & Butter
with BACON, HAM or SAUSAGE

VIRGINIA HAM
SHELL STEAK 6.05
2 EGGS Potatoes & Toast
PASTRAMI & 2 EGGS 6.35
POTATOES & TOAST
SALAMI & 2 EGGS 5.25
POTATOES & TOAST

Magnets $3.00

RESTAURANT

MATZO BREI

This is how my grandmother made this traditional recipe that's like a scrambled French toast made from matzo crackers. It is eaten especially during Passover to celebrate the emancipation of the slaves. Power to the people!

SERVES 2

Preparation time: 15 minutes
Cooking time: 10 minutes

INGREDIENTS

4 matzos
4 eggs
½ cup milk
½ teaspoon ground cinnamon
1 pinch salt
1 teaspoon sugar
3 tablespoons butter
2 tablespoons neutral/unflavored
   cooking oil

PREPARATION

With your hands, break the matzos up into bite-sized pieces. Soak the broken matzos in cold water for 5 minutes. While the matzos are soaking, combine the other ingredients, except the butter and oil, in a bowl, mixing with a fork or whisk. Drain the soaked matzos in a colander, then place them in the egg–milk batter and let them soak until most or all of the mixture has been absorbed. Drain off any excess liquid in a colander.

COOKING

In a frying pan, heat the butter and oil over medium heat—you want enough to just cover the surface. When the butter and oil start to sizzle, add the matzo mixture, spreading it out so that it is no more than one or two layers thick. Depending on the size of your pan, you may need to cook it in batches. Flip and separate the matzo so it's slightly golden and scrambled on both sides. This takes about 5 minutes.
Serve hot with jam or other sweet toppings. Personally, I like to mix in obscene amounts of jam.

CHOCOLATE RUGELACHS

You'll enjoy making these cute little twists as much as eating them.

MAKES 12 CRESCENTS

Preparation time: 30 minutes, plus cooling
Resting time: 4 hours
Cooking time: about 20 minutes

DOUGH

⅔ cup all-purpose flour
¼ cup plain cream cheese, softened
¼ cup sweet/unsalted butter, softened
2 pinches salt

GANACHE

2 tablespoons whipping cream
2 teaspoons unsalted butter
2¼ oz dark chocolate, broken into pieces

TOPPING

1¾ oz dark chocolate, finely chopped
¼ cup superfine sugar

GLAZE

1 egg yolk
1 teaspoon water

TOPPING (JAM VERSION)

3 teaspoons sugar
1 teaspoon ground cinnamon (optional)

THE DOUGH

Using a food processor or by hand, mix the dough ingredients until combined. Wrap in plastic wrap and refrigerate for at least 4 hours.

THE GANACHE

In a saucepan, heat the cream and butter over medium heat until they come to a boil. Add the pieces of chocolate. Take off the heat and let it melt for 1 minute. Stir with a spatula until smooth and even.

SHAPING THE DOUGH

Preheat the oven to 325°F. On a floured work surface, roll out the dough with a rolling pin to make a round about 12 inches in diameter. Spread the ganache with a spatula over the whole round. Mix together the topping ingredients and scatter over the ganache, setting some aside for sprinkling on top. Cut the round into 12 equal wedges, like a pie, and roll each one up, starting with the wider end, to make a small crescent. Place the completed crescents, as you make them, on a baking sheet lined with parchment paper.

THE GLAZING

Brush the rugelachs with the mixture of egg yolk and water. Sprinkle over the reserved chocolate–sugar topping.

COOKING

Bake in the oven for about 20 minutes until the crescents are golden brown. Allow to cool for at least 10 minutes before serving.

TO MAKE JAM RUGELACHS

Replace the ganache and chocolate topping with ½ cup jam (apricot or raspberry work well), and 2¾ oz nuts (pine nuts or pistachios, depending on your taste) and sprinkle the rugelachs with the mixture of sugar and cinnamon.

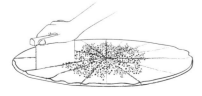

FRENCH TOAST

French toast is one of the first things I learned to cook as a child. When I would go to a diner with my mother for breakfast, she would always ask them to make it well soaked.

SERVES 2

Preparation time: 10 minutes
Cooking time: 5 minutes

INGREDIENTS

about ⅓ loaf challah (page 14)
4 eggs
5 tablespoons milk
5 tablespoons whipping cream
3 drops natural vanilla extract
½ teaspoon ground cinnamon
1 pinch salt
2 teaspoons sugar
3 tablespoons butter or 2 tablespoons
    neutral cooking oil
maple syrup and butter, to serve

PREPARATION

Cut the challah into ¾–1¼ inch slices. The loaf can be fresh, but slightly stale is even better. Mix all of the other ingredients, except the butter or oil, with a fork or a whisk until combined. Soak the bread in this mixture for a few minutes on each side until the slices are fully saturated.

COOKING AND SERVING

Brown the soaked slices in a frying pan over medium heat in the butter or oil for 2–3 minutes each side. The slices should be golden on the outside but still moist on the inside.
Serve with maple syrup and butter.

tip: In my opinion, French toast made with challah is the best, but a good sandwich bread or brioche works well.

RICE CRISPY TREATS

This all-American classic was invented by Kellogg's® and is usually made using Rice Krispies® and store-bought marshmallows. Making them with homemade marshmallows and organic puffed rice are two ways to improve on the original.

MAKES 16 SQUARES

Preparation time: 10 minutes, plus cooling
Cooking time: 5 minutes

INGREDIENTS

5 tablespoons sweet/unsalted butter
1 lb 5 oz marshmallows (page 232)
2 pinches salt
12 cups puffed rice (Rice Krispies®, or other)

THE MIXTURE

Oil or butter a square 9½ inch cake pan. Melt the butter, marshmallows, and salt in a pan over low heat. Be careful not to overcook the mixture; stop the cooking as soon as the butter and marshmallows have melted. Mix the melted marshmallows and butter with the puffed rice in a large bowl.

SETTING AND SERVING

Using a spatula, transfer everything to the pan, pressing just enough to get the mixture well distributed but being careful not to crush the puffed rice.
Allow to cool and cut into squares.

tip: You can also add twists to this recipe, like chocolate chips, seeds, or nuts.

BLINTZES

I used to devour these Ashkenazi-style filled pancakes at my grandmother's in Brooklyn.
My two favorite fillings were cheese and blueberries.

MAKES 12 BLINTZ

Preparation time: 30 minutes
Resting time: 1 hour
Cooking time: 40 minutes

DRY INGREDIENTS

1⅔ cups all-purpose flour
3 pinches salt
2 teaspoons superfine sugar

WET INGREDIENTS

1¼ cups milk
¾ cup water
3 tablespoons sweet/unsalted
    butter, melted
4 eggs

CHEESE FILLING

1 lb ricotta cheese
½ cup superfine sugar
3 egg whites
4½ teaspoons cornstarch

BLUEBERRY FILLING

2 tablespoons sweet/unsalted butter
1 lb 2 oz blueberries
⅓ cup superfine sugar
4½ teaspoons cornstarch
sour cream, for topping

THE BATTER

Combine the dry ingredients. Whisk together the wet ingredients vigorously, then add the dry mixture while beating until combined. You need to let the batter rest for at least 1 hour before cooking. If possible, make it the night before and keep it in the refrigerator.

THE CHEESE FILLING

Combine the ingredients for the cheese filling with a fork. Cook the filling in a saucepan over low heat, stirring constantly for 10 minutes or until you have a consistency similar to mashed potato.

THE BLUEBERRY FILLING

Melt the butter in a pan over medium heat. Combine the blueberries, sugar, and cornstarch, and cook in the butter for 5 minutes or until it has thickened.

COOKING AND SERVING

Heat a little oil in a frying pan over medium heat. Pour and spread a ladle of batter in the hot frying pan. When the bottom begins to brown, turn the blintz with a spatula. Spread about 2 tablespoons of filling in the middle of the blintz, fold in the edges, and roll the blintz to enclose the filling. Keep cooking the blintz on both sides—it should be golden brown all over. Serve hot with sour cream.

11 : 28

BRUNCH TIME

BAGELS

This iconic wheel-shaped bread was first brought to New York by Jewish immigrants from Eastern Europe. Authentic, fresh, bagels are still quite rare outside of New York, which is why some of us like to make our own.

MAKES 10 BAGELS
Preparation time: 40 minutes
Resting time: 1 hour
Cooking time: 45 minutes

DRY INGREDIENTS
5 cups bread flour
1½ teaspoons dried yeast
3 teaspoons salt

WET INGREDIENTS
1½ cups lukewarm water
    (or 1¾ cups if you add the
    wheat gluten, see note)
2 tablespoons malt syrup
    or sugar syrup
1½ tablespoons olive oil

POACHING INGREDIENTS
3 teaspoons potato flour
12 cups water
3 teaspoons malt syrup
    or simple syrup
1½ teaspoons salt

TOPPING (OPTIONAL)
sesame seeds and poppy seeds are
    the most traditional, but you
    can experiment with other things

THE DOUGH
Combine the dry ingredients, and beat together the wet ingredients. Combine the two mixtures and knead vigorously for about 10 minutes until the dough is smooth and elastic.
Divide the dough into 10 equal portions and form into small balls.

SHAPING THE DOUGH
Using the palms of your hands, flatten and stretch the balls of dough to make sausages 8–10 inches long. Flatten one of the ends into a hook shape. Wrap it around the other end and pinch to seal. Place each bagel on an individual square of parchment paper to make it easier to move them later. Scatter over some flour, then cover with plastic wrap, and allow them to rise at room temperature for 1 hour.

COOKING
Preheat the oven to 450°F. If it is an electric oven, place a bowl of water in the bottom of the oven 15 minutes before baking. Blend the potato flour into 1 cup of the cold water, then dissolve it with the rest of the poaching ingredients in a large saucepan. Bring to a rolling boil and then lower the heat so the water is just simmering. Drop the bagels into the water, in batches if necessary. After about 1 minute, turn them over, and cook for another 30 seconds. Take them out using a slotted spoon and place them on a baking sheet lined with parchment paper. Finally, sprinkle the topping over the damp bagels. Place the sheet of bagels in the oven, lower the temperature to 415°F and bake for 20–25 minutes until the bagels start to brown.

note: If you can't find bread flour, which is a high gluten flour, you can use all-purpose flour with the addition of 1½ tablespoons wheat gluten (available from health food stores).

CHICKEN SALAD SANDWICH

This has a traditional Mexican avocado spread which replaces the usual mayonnaise in a chicken salad.

MAKES 2 SANDWICHES

Preparation time: 15 minutes

SANDWICHES

2 bagels (page 72)

GUACAMOLE

1 small ripe avocado, halved, stone
   removed, and peeled

1½ oz red onion, finely chopped

½ lime

2 pinches salt + 1 turn of the
   pepper mill

1 pinch ground cumin

1–2 drops of hot pepper sauce
   (optional)

FILLING

10½ oz leftover roast chicken
   (page 142)

4 slices of tomato

1 handful arugula

2 pinches salt + 2 turns
   of the pepper mill

THE GUACAMOLE

Crush the avocado with a fork. Add the chopped red onion to the mashed avocado, squeeze the half lime, and add the juice to the mixture. Season with the salt and pepper, and add the cumin and hot pepper sauce, if using.

THE FILLING AND ASSEMBLY

Chop the leftover chicken into small pieces. Add them to the guacamole. Combine gently.

Slice the bagels in half horizontally, then top the bottom half of each bagel with the chicken–guacamole mixture. Add two slices of tomato to each sandwich and divide the handful of greens. Season with the salt and pepper. Cover with the top half of the bagel and enjoy immediately.

DILL POTATO SALAD

See recipe page 114.

SMOKED SALMON BAGEL

The classic New York breakfast sandwich as sold at fine establishments like Murray's Sturgeon Shop on the Upper West Side of Manhattan. Nothing can beat it!

MAKES 2 SANDWICHES

Preparation time: 5 minutes

INGREDIENTS

2 bagels (page 72)
2¾ oz plain cream cheese
7 oz smoked salmon
2 slices white onion (optional)
6 thin slices of tomato

Slice the bagels in half horizontally. You can toast them if you want to, but normally, if they are fresh, it's not worth the trouble.

Spread both halves with a thick layer of cream cheese and, on the bottom half, add in order: Smoked salmon, one slice white onion, if using, and two or three thin slices of tomato. Top with the other half of the bagel, and cut in two before serving.

BIALYS

While the bagel is boiled and baked, its lesser known cousin, the bialy, is just baked. The other big difference is that the bialy only has a hollow in the middle while the bagel has a hole.

MAKES 6 BIALYS

Preparation time: 25 minutes
Resting time: 2½ hours
Cooking time: 15 minutes

DOUGH

2⅔ cups bread flour
1½ teaspoons dried yeast
3 teaspoons salt
1 cup lukewarm water
3 teaspoons olive oil

COOKING SHEET

1 tablespoon butter
2 pinches fine cornmeal

FILLING

1½ tablespoons olive oil
5½ oz onion, finely chopped
1 teaspoon poppy seeds
1 teaspoon salt

THE DOUGH

Mix together the flour, yeast, and salt. In a bowl, beat the lukewarm water and olive oil. Incorporate the first mixture into the second and knead vigorously by hand, or using an electric mixer, for 10 minutes, until the dough is smooth and elastic.

Form a smooth ball of dough. Place the dough in an oiled bowl, cover with plastic wrap and let it rest at room temperature for about 1½ hours until the dough has doubled in size.

SHAPING THE DOUGH

Divide the dough into six equal portions. Shape into small balls and flatten them between the palms of your hands. Place the rounds of dough on a buttered and floured sheet of parchment paper. Fold the opposite edges of each dough portion towards the middle and pinch together to make irregular balls. Sprinkle with flour, then cover loosely with plastic wrap. Let them rise at room temperature for at least 1 hour.

Using the palm of your hand, flatten the risen balls of dough, then press the middle of each bialy to make a large hollow.

THE FILLING

Heat the olive oil in a frying pan, and sauté the onions and poppy seeds over medium heat. Season with the salt.

Put a little of the onion–poppy seed mixture in the middle of each bialy and brush the surface of the bialys with more olive oil. Don't worry if the onion mixture spills out, bialys should be imperfect!

COOKING

Preheat the oven to 425°F. Grease a baking sheet with the butter, and sprinkle with the cornmeal. Place the bialys in the middle or upper part of the oven and bake for about 10 minutes until they're lightly browned.

MACKEREL BIALYS

In New York, this sandwich filling is made using white fish,
but in France I use smoked mackerel, which is technically
a "blue" fish. I can guarantee it's just as good.

MAKES 3 BIALYS

Preparation time: 20 minutes
Refrigeration time: at least
    30 minutes

SANDWICHES

3 bialys (page 78)

FILLING

5½ oz smoked, cooked blue fish
    (mackerel or "bloater" herring)
1¾ oz fennel and/or celery,
    finely chopped
1 oz onion, finely chopped
2 tablespoons sour cream
1 tablespoon plain mayonnaise
    (page 264)
1 pinch salt + 1 turn of the
    pepper mill

ASSEMBLY

6 lettuce leaves (cos/romaine
    or butter lettuce)
½ cucumber, sliced very thinly
    or the equivalent amount
    of sweet pickles (see "fast pickles,"
    page 242)

THE FILLING

Remove the skin from the fish and lift the flesh from the bones.
Add the fennel and/or celery, onion, sour cream, and mayonnaise.
Season with the salt and pepper, and gently combine. Place in the
refrigerator for at least 30 minutes.

THE ASSEMBLY

Slice the bialys in two. Cover the bottom half of each bialy with
two lettuce leaves, then add the blue fish filling. Top with the
slices of cucumber or pickle and the other half of each bialy.
Enjoy immediately.

COLESLAW

See recipe page 265.

KATZ'S

In the 1930s, the golden age of Yiddish theater on Manhattan's Lower East Side, this Jewish delicatessen was the place to be seen. Today, with its inimitable corned beef sandwiches and its knishes, it remains an indispensable institution for locals and tourists alike.

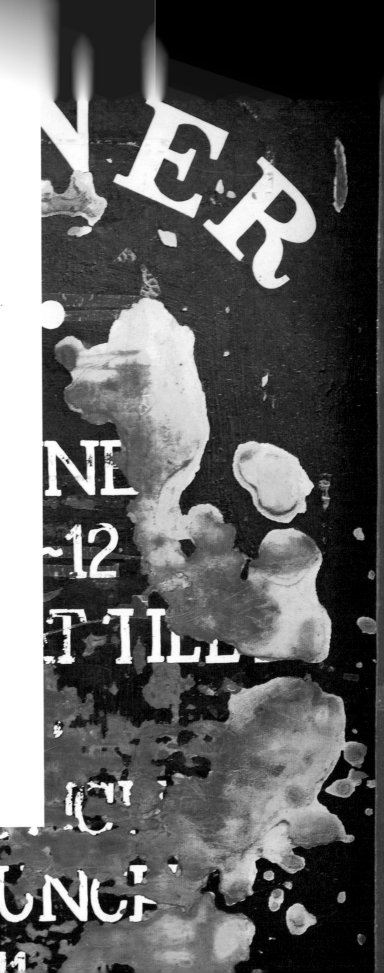

EGGS
OVER EASY

These are sunny-side up eggs
that are briefly flipped over.

SERVES 1
Preparation time: 5 minutes
Cooking time: 5 minutes

INGREDIENTS
2½ tablespoons sweet/unsalted butter or olive oil
2 eggs

THE EGGS
Heat the butter or olive oil, or a combination of the
two, over medium heat in a (truly) nonstick frying
pan. When the butter or olive oil starts to sizzle,
carefully crack the eggs into the frying pan.
After a couple of minutes, use a wide, thin, clean
spatula to make sure that the eggs are completely
unstuck from the bottom of the frying pan, gently
sliding it under the eggs to loosen any sticky spots.
Now tilt the pan to slide an egg onto the spatula
(jiggling the spatula forward if necessary) and then
gently flip the egg over at the edge of the frying pan
(don't drop it!). Repeat with the other egg. After
20 seconds or so, tilt the pan to slide the eggs onto
the edge of a plate. Season. If you practice enough,
making eggs this way will eventually come naturally.
Along the way, you can consider eggs over easy as
an exercise in gentleness.

PAN-FRIED BACON
See recipe page 88.

HASH BROWNS
See recipe page 86.

HASH BROWNS

Pan-fried shredded potatoes.

SERVES 2

Preparation time: 10 minutes
Cooking time: 20 minutes

INGREDIENTS

14 oz russet potatoes
   (about 2 large potatoes)
1 cup cooking oil

PREPARING THE POTATOES

Peel the potatoes and shred them with a hand shredder, or the shredder attachment of a food processor. Over a sieve (to catch any pieces that fall), squeeze the potatoes by hand to extract as much water as possible.

COOKING

To a small frying pan over medium heat, add enough oil to come to ¼ inch and heat until sizzling. Add enough potato to completely fill the frying pan with a layer about ½ inch thick. The exact amount will depend on the size of the frying pan. Use a spatula to spread out the potato evenly, then gently push down on the edge of the potato, which naturally contract to a semisolid flapjack.

After about 5 minutes, when the underside is golden brown, use a wide spatula to flip the potato over. The smaller the frying pan, the more likely you will be able to flip all of the potato in one piece. Continue cooking for a further 5 minutes until the second side is golden brown. Place the hash browns on paper towels or a wire rack to drain off excess oil, then repeat with the remaining potato and oil.

SERVING

You can keep the hash browns warm in an oven preheated to 200°F. Season with salt and pepper.

CHARCOAL PRIME STEAKS & RIBS

DISCOVER MasterCard VISA AMERICAN EXPRESS

BIG NICK'S JOINTS HAVE BEEN FEATURE

- DAILY NEWS
- NEW YORK MAG. (GAEL GREENE)
- GOOD HOUSEK'G
- TV SHOPPER

- ABC-TV NEWS
- WOR-RADIO (JOAN HAMBURG)
- NY ON $60 A DAY.

- N.Y. TIM
- NEW. DA
- WESTSID
- "MIDNIGH COW

SMOKED BACON

I love smoked bacon in the morning. The smell alone (especially when combined with coffee) is reason enough to wake up. And somehow it just seems to blend perfectly with whatever else I'm having for breakfast—whether it's something purely savory like eggs and potatoes, or something sweeter like flapjacks or French toast, where my favorite thing is to let the crispy, salty, bacon steep in the maple syrup. I like to cook it a few different ways but, regardless of method, I would advise you to get the best quality meat you can afford, as it will make all the difference.

PAN-FRIED BACON

This is the method I use when I'm making bacon for just a few people, or when using an oven is impractical.

Lay the strips of bacon side by side in a cold, nonstick frying pan. Heat over medium heat and after a few minutes, when the bacon naturally comes unstuck from the base of the pan, turn the slices using chopsticks or tongs. Continue cooking and turning until the bacon is as crispy as you like it. Drain on paper towels and serve.

OVEN-BAKED BACON

This is a better method if you need to make a lot of bacon in one shot. The crispness of the bacon is also more even, and it's not as messy as cooking it in the frying pan.

Preheat the oven to 400°F. Place the slices of bacon side by side on a baking sheet (lined with parchment paper or unlined). Bake for about 15 minutes until the bacon is as crispy as you like it.

CANDIED BACON

Oven-baked bacon with an indulgent twist.

Preheat the oven to 315°F. Line a baking sheet with parchment paper.

Pour some superfine sugar onto a wide plate. Coat the bacon with the sugar by laying it on the sugar on the plate, one strip at a time, and flipping it over with your fingers. Lay the sugar-coated strips of bacon on the parchment paper and bake for 25–30 minutes, checking regularly that the sugar isn't burning. Serve hot or warm.

HUEVOS RANCHEROS

In Brooklyn, you can find an excellent rendition of this Mexican breakfast dish at one of the La Esquina restaurants. To recreate an authentic experience in Paris, I turned to my personal expert on all things Mexican, who also happens to be my business partner, Amaury de Veyrac.

SERVES 2

Preparation time: 45 minutes
Cooking time: 35 minutes

TORTILLAS (MAKES 10)

1 cup all-purpose flour
1 cup fine cornmeal or replace with
    the same quantity of wheat flour
¾ cup lukewarm water

TOMATO SALSA

1 small red onion, finely chopped
2 tomatoes, seeded and chopped
1 pinch dried oregano
1 teaspoon sugar
1 garlic clove, finely chopped
1 jalapeño pepper or 1 pinch red
    chili powder

EGGS AND TOPPING

4 tablespoons canned black beans,
    rinsed (optional)
1 pinch salt
2 eggs
3½ oz Monterey Jack cheese,
    finely shredded
1 lime
1 avocado, chopped (optional)
4 sprigs cilantro, roughly chopped

THE TORTILLA DOUGH

Combine the flour and cornmeal in a bowl. Add the water gradually while working the mixture until you have a firm dough. Continue to knead the dough on a floured surface. When you have a ball of dough that's nice and smooth, divide it into 10 equal portions and roll them out on the floured surface, making the tortillas as thin as possible. (You can use a tortilla press if available.)

COOKING THE TORTILLAS

Heat a nonstick frying pan over high heat and cook the tortillas for about 1 minute on each side. You should have some brown marks on both sides. Stack the ones that are ready between two sheets of foil to prevent them from drying out.

THE TOMATO SALSA

Lightly sauté the onion in a saucepan in a little sunflower oil over medium heat. Add the remaining ingredients, season with salt and pepper, then reduce the heat to low. Cover and cook, stirring occasionally, for 15 minutes. Place in a food processor or blender, and process until a chunky salsa forms.

EGGS AND TOPPING

If you choose the black beans option, heat them up with the salt in a saucepan, then mash them with a fork. Keep them warm in the oven, covered.
Fry two to four tortillas (depending on how hungry you are) with sunflower oil in a frying pan over high heat for about 2 minutes on each side (you can freeze the others, wrapped in plastic wrap). Fry the eggs in the same frying pan and scatter over three-quarters of the cheese. Juice the lime.

ASSEMBLY

On each plate, place the egg on the warm tortilla with the tomato salsa (around the yolk), a few pieces of avocado, if using, the mashed black beans, if using, chopped cilantro, the rest of the cheese, and a little lime juice. *Buen provecho!*

OMELET

What I like in an omelet is a soft tubular form (not just a circle folded in half), a moist yellow (not dry and broiled) surface, and a slightly wet (but not uncooked) interior. After this, there is no limit to what can go inside.

MAKES 1 OMELET

Preparation time: 10 minutes
Cooking time: 20 minutes

FILLING

2 tablespoons butter
1 large handful baby spinach
1 large handful mushrooms, sliced
3 teaspoons pine nuts
½ cup creamy goat cheese,
    crumbled

OMELET

3 or 4 eggs
1 tablespoon milk
1 pinch salt
1 teaspoon dried herbs or fresh
    herbs, chopped (optional)
1½ oz butter or 2 tablespoons
    sunflower oil

THE FILLING

This is a filling that I often make at home: Baby spinach with pine nuts, cheese, and fried mushrooms.
Heat the butter in a frying pan over medium heat, then sweat the spinach, and brown the mushrooms separately, discarding the liquid released from the vegetables each time. When cooked, place them in a bowl together. Toast the pine nuts for 1–2 minutes until golden, and add to the mushrooms and spinach. Add the crumbled goat cheese.

THE OMELET

Whisk together all the omelet ingredients, except the butter or oil, until all of the ingredients are very well combined. Melt the butter or oil over low–medium heat in a nonstick frying pan, and pour in the eggs. It is absolutely essential that the eggs not stick to the bottom of the frying pan, which is why I advise a generous portion of butter or oil, and insist on a truly nonstick frying pan. But feel free to cut down on the fat if you know that your pan doesn't need it. Using a spatula, move the eggs in a folding motion almost as if making scrambled eggs, tilting the frying pan as you do this so that liquid egg will fill in the empty spaces created by the spatula. The idea is to evenly cook the eggs on a low–medium heat so you don't have an omelet that's overcooked (too dark) on the outside and/or undercooked inside. After a few minutes, when the eggs have mostly thickened but are still visibly wet, tilt the frying pan one last time to fill any holes, and add your filling in a strip across the omelet, at about the one-third mark of the omelet circle.

THE FOLDING

Allow the eggs to set for a minute or so before using the spatula to check whether they're cooked enough to hold together when folding. When this is the case (before the eggs have dried out), fold the omelet around the filling to form a tube and slide onto a plate.

HASH BROWNS

See recipe page 86.

EGGS BENEDICT

Legend has it that a guest at the Waldorf Astoria hotel in New York invented eggs Benedict in the hope of easing his hangover. While off-the-shelf hollandaise sauces are readily available, I encourage you to make your own. It will make all the difference.

SERVES 6

Preparation time: 20 minutes
Cooking time: 25 minutes

HOLLANDAISE SAUCE

2 egg yolks
1 teaspoon lemon juice
1 teaspoon white wine
½ cup sweet/unsalted butter (preferably clarified), melted

EGGS

12 eggs
white vinegar or rice vinegar
12–24 bacon slices
6 English muffins (page 96)
⅓ cup butter
cayenne pepper (optional)

THE SAUCE

Bring a saucepan of water to a boil and turn off the heat. In a large bowl, whisk the egg yolks, lemon juice, and wine (or water) until the mixture has thickened noticeably. Place the bowl over the saucepan of hot water and slowly pour in the melted butter while whisking constantly to form an emulsion that should be a bit less thick than a mayonnaise. Keep the bowl over the warm water until you're ready to serve. If the sauce becomes too thick, whisk in a little hot water to thin it out.

THE POACHED EGGS

If you don't have an egg poacher, you can poach your eggs the old-fashioned way. Bring 4–8 cups of water to a boil in a large saucepan, then turn the heat down to a simmer. Add a little vinegar to help the eggs coagulate (1–2 tablespoons to 4 cups of water). Carefully break an egg into a small cup or bowl and slide it slowly into the water—the aim being to keep the egg white from spreading all over the place. Use a spatula to nudge the white around the yolk. When the white is set (i.e. no longer transparent), but before it is hard and pale, remove the poached egg with a slotted spoon. Poached eggs that are not being served immediately can be removed from the water slightly undercooked and kept in a bowl of iced water until ready to serve. They can then be reheated in gently simmering water for about 20 seconds.

THE MEAT

Round, so-called "Canadian," bacon is traditional, but feel free to use any other cured meats, such as smoked bacon. In any case, brown it in a frying pan over medium heat for a few minutes on each side until it is as crispy as you like it. Another popular twist is to replace the meat with a mixture of smoked salmon and cooked Swiss chard.

ASSEMBLY

Toast the English muffins and spread with butter. Lay one or two slices of bacon on top, then the eggs. Pour over some sauce and sprinkle with cayenne pepper.

POTATOES

See "home fries" recipe page 265.

ENGLISH MUFFINS

My baker friend Gavin Smart was kind enough to share his recipe for English muffins.

MAKES 10 MUFFINS
Preparation time: 30 minutes
Resting time: about 3 hours
Cooking time: 30 minutes

SOURDOUGH STARTER
MAKES 3 PORTIONS
Preparation time: 20 minutes
Resting time: about 2½ days

PREPARATION 1
3 tablespoons lukewarm water
⅓ cup whole-wheat flour

PREPARATION 2
¼ cup water
⅔ cup all-purpose flour
1 tablespoon superfine sugar

PREPARATION 3
1⅓ cups all-purpose flour
¾ cup water

INGREDIENTS
3 tablespoons sugar
2 cups water (at around 105°F)
1 oz fresh yeast
1 portion (8½ oz) sourdough starter
5¼–6⅔ cups all-purpose flour
½ cup powdered milk
¼ cup sweet/unsalted butter,
    softened
3 teaspoons salt
semolina flour, for dusting

SOURDOUGH STARTER
Whisk together the ingredients for the first preparation in a bowl, cover with plastic wrap, and leave to ferment for a day at room temperature. Whisk together the second preparation ingredients in the same way, add it to the first preparation, and mix again. Cover with plastic wrap and let it ferment for another day. Whisk together the third preparation ingredients as for the others, add it to the sourdough starter, and mix again. Cover with plastic wrap and let it ferment for half a day. Your starter is now ready to use.

THE DOUGH
In a bowl, dissolve the sugar in the water, then add the yeast, one portion of sourdough starter and 1 cup flour. Whisk them together and let the mixture ferment for 2–3 minutes. Add the powdered milk powder, butter, salt, and another cup of the flour, and mix well. Continue to add the flour and combine until you have a dough that holds together well and comes away from the bowl. Tip the dough onto your work surface and knead for about 8 minutes until it is quite smooth but not too stiff. Add a little flour if necessary. Scrape out your mixing bowl, then lightly oil it with a little vegetable oil and place the dough inside. Cover with plastic wrap and allow it to rise at room temperature for about 2 hours until it has doubled in size.

SHAPING THE DOUGH
When the dough has doubled in size, punch it down to release the air, and turn it out onto a floured work surface. Let it rest for a few minutes, then divide it into two pieces. Roll out each piece to a thickness of ⅝ inch and cut out circles using a 3½ inch round cutter. Dust two or three baking sheets with semolina flour and place the circles of dough on top. Scatter over some more semolina flour, cover with plastic wrap, and allow them to rise for about 1 hour.

COOKING
Preheat the oven to 350°F. Heat a frying pan over medium heat and carefully transfer three or four muffins to the frying pan, depending on the size of your pan (don't add too many at once). Cook them for 5–10 minutes on each side until they have a good color. Finish the cooking in the oven for another 5 minutes to make sure they are cooked right through.

tip: Keep your sourdough starter in an airtight container in the refrigerator for 5–7 days. After that, you need to refresh it with equal quantities of hot water and flour. For example, ¼ cup hot water for ⅔ cup all-purpose flour. Take the starter out of the refrigerator, mix as above, and let it ferment a little while before returning it to the refrigerator.

12 : 42
LUNCH TIME

BUNS FOR HAMBURGERS & HOT DOGS

For a great burger or a hot dog, the bun is at least as important as what you put in it. The real test for a bun is being good enough to eat by itself. These are.

MAKES 10 HAMBURGER BUNS OR 10 HOT DOG BUNS

Preparation time: 25 minutes
Resting time: about 2½ hours
Cooking time: 11–12 minutes

DRY INGREDIENTS

4½ cups all-purpose flour
2 teaspoons dried yeast
3 tablespoons superfine sugar
2 teaspoons salt

WET INGREDIENTS

⅔ cup water
3 tablespoons butter
¾ cup milk
4 egg yolks

GLAZE

1½ tablespoons milk
sesame seeds (optional)

THE DOUGH

Combine all the dry ingredients. Heat the water and butter in a saucepan until the butter is melted. Remove from the heat and add the milk. Check the temperature of the mixture with a thermometer—it needs to be 120–130°F.

Combine the two mixtures. Start kneading and add the egg yolks one at a time, kneading well after each addition. Keep kneading until the dough is very elastic (10 minutes in an electric mixer, 10–20 minutes by hand).

Form a smooth ball of dough, place it in an oiled container and cover with plastic wrap. Let it rise for about 1½ hours at room temperature until it has doubled in volume.

SHAPING AND THE SECOND RISE

Divide the dough into 10 equal portions.

For hamburger buns, shape the portions into balls between the palms of your hands and place them in round buttered and floured molds, about 4½ inches in diameter and ¾ inch high.

For hot dog buns, form the balls into torpedo shapes—ideally, tubes about 4½ inches long and 1½ inches across—and put them in buttered and floured elongated molds, or a homemade equivalent made out of foil.

Place the molds on a baking sheet. Sprinkle with flour, then cover loosely with plastic wrap. Let them rise for at least 1 hour at room temperature until they have doubled in volume.

COOKING

Preheat the oven to 425°F. Glaze the buns by brushing them with the milk, but be careful not to crush them. Sprinkle with sesame seeds, if using. Cook the buns in the oven for 11–12 minutes until they're golden brown. The undersides should be lightly colored.

CHEESEBURGER

It's easy to make a burger that's just okay. Taking your patties and hamburgers to the next level demands a little more effort, but it's really worth it. Here are the basic rules.

MAKES 2 CHEESEBURGERS

Preparation time: 15 minutes
Cooking time: 10 minutes

INGREDIENTS

7 oz ground meat (see note)
2 slices cheese (cheddar, Gruyére, Swiss …)
2 buns (page 102)
6 rounds pickled onion or other pickles (page 242)
lettuce and/or tomato
⅓ cup sauce (ketchup, mayonnaise, special sauce)

SPECIAL SAUCE

½ cup mayonnaise
3 teaspoons ketchup
1 teaspoon mustard
1 teaspoon sweet pickles, finely chopped
1 teaspoon hot pepper sauce (optional)

note: *The possible meat combinations are endless, you can even add pork, lamb, etc. What's key is that your ground meat should not be too lean —it should contain 15–25 % fat.*

THE MEAT AND CHEESE

It's important to resist the temptation to press the meat into perfect compact pucks like the ready-made ones from the supermarket, or the ones shaped by the butcher. Burgers cook better when they are loosely put together, so you should work them with your hands and without pressing too hard. A good portion size is about 3½ oz, though it can be smaller.
Brown the meat in a little butter or oil in a nonstick frying pan over medium–high heat, turning only once if possible. Gently press the meat with a spatula. After 3–5 minutes, when the first side is well browned, turn over the burger, and cook the other side for 3–5 minutes. The temperature of the inside of the meat should be 140–160°F, according to taste. Check for doneness by pressing the patty with your fingers: The denser it feels, the more cooked it is. For a cheeseburger, add a slice or two of cheese on the browned side of the burger once it has been turned over. The cheese will melt while the meat continues to cook.

TOPPINGS AND BUNS

Make the toppings in advance. They might be lettuce, tomatoes, pickles (pickled onions, for example), and a sauce, such as ketchup (page 264), mayonnaise (page 264), or a special sauce, which is usually a mixture of different condiments.
Slice the buns in half and toast them just before starting to cook the meat so they are still warm when you serve the burger. You can toast them in a frying pan with a little butter, but this is optional.

ASSEMBLY

Spread the sauce on the bottom half of the toasted bun and put the cooked burger on top, followed by the other toppings, such as lettuce or tomato. You can put sliced pickles under or on top of the meat.

THE PICKLED ONIONS

See "fast pickles" recipe page 242.

FRENCH FRIES

See recipe page 128.

VEGGIE BURGER

A good vegetarian burger should be as fully satisfying for a meat eater
as for a vegetarian. This is a patty recipe I've been fiddling with for years.

MAKES 4 BURGERS
Preparation time: 25 minutes
Cooking time: 45 minutes

TO COOK
½ cup pearl barley (or a little more,
    given that volumes can vary)

TO SAUTÉ
3 teaspoons finely chopped onion
½ oz mushrooms, thinly sliced
3 teaspoons cooking oil
2 pinches sweet or smoked paprika
    (optional)

OTHER INGREDIENTS
2 egg whites
6 oz can red kidney beans,
    drained and rinsed
3 medjool dates, pitted
1 tablespoon cornstarch
2 tablespoons diced beets,
    preferably raw
3 teaspoons soy sauce
2 pinches light brown sugar
2 tablespoons Italian flat leaf parsley
1 teaspoon salt

COOKING THE PEARL BARLEY
The ½ cup of barley plus three times its volume in water should give you about 1½ cups of cooked barley, but to be safe you could cook a little more. Boil the water with the barley, then lower the heat, and simmer for about 30 minutes. If, when the water is absorbed, the barley is still too hard, add more water and keep cooking until the barley is as tender as you like it. If, on the other hand, the barley is tender before all the water is absorbed, turn off the heat and drain off the excess water. Cool.

SAUTÉING THE VEGETABLES
Sauté the onions and mushrooms in the oil for about 5 minutes until the onions are translucent. Add the paprika to finish.

THE PATTIES
Process the sautéed vegetables and the cooked barley with the other ingredients in a food processor, then, using wet hands, shape the mixture into 4 burgers.
In a frying pan, cook the burgers in some oil over low heat, 5–7 minutes on each side until nicely browned, then turn them over carefully with a wide, thin spatula. For uniformly shaped burgers, use a round cutter filled to three-quarters in the frying pan. Remove it before turning over the burger.

THE BURGER
Serve on buns with sauce and toppings as for meat hamburgers (page 104).

SWEET POTATOES
See "home fries" recipe page 265.

EGGPLANT BURGER

This is a hybrid of two of my favorite New York sandwiches:
The diner "pizza burger" and the traditional Italian "eggplant Parmesan sub."

SERVES 2

Preparation time: 20 minutes
Resting time: 30 minutes
Cooking time: 20 minutes

PATTIES

1 eggplant
2 teaspoons salt
1 cup all-purpose flour
1 egg
1 teaspoon milk
1⅓ cups dry breadcrumbs
1 teaspoon dried oregano
1 teaspoon dried basil
¼ cup cooking oil (add more
    if needed)

OTHER INGREDIENTS

9 oz fresh mozzarella cheese, sliced
1 oz Parmesan cheese, grated
1 cup tomato sauce (page 166)
2 buns (page 102)

THE PATTIES

Cut the eggplant into slices about ½ inch thick. Sprinkle with the salt and let them drain in a colander for 30 minutes. Dry the slices on paper towels. Have a bowl ready with the flour. In another bowl, beat the egg with the milk. In a third bowl, combine the breadcrumbs and the dried herbs. Heat about ¾ inch of oil in a fairly deep frying pan over medium heat. First dip the slices of eggplant in the flour, then in the egg, and finally in the breadcrumbs. Fry in the oil for a few minutes until golden on each side and drain on paper towels. Preheat the oven to 415°F.

COOKING AND ASSEMBLY

On a baking sheet lined with parchment paper, put together four stacks (one per half bun), alternating slices of eggplant and the two kinds of cheese, sometimes putting a little tomato sauce under the cheese. Bake for a few minutes until the cheese starts to bubble.
While the stacks are cooking, open the hamburger buns and toast them in a little butter in a frying pan until lightly browned.
On a serving plate, cover the cut sides of the buns with tomato sauce. Place the cooked eggplant stacks on top. Insert a toothpick to hold the burgers together.

GREEK SALAD

See recipe page 112.

GREEK SALAD

In terms of Greek salad, the benchmark for me is the generous version served at Big Nick's joint on the Upper West Side of Manhattan, where it comes with a dressing full of crunch.

SERVES 4

Preparation time: 20 minutes
Refrigeration time: 30 minutes

DRESSING

3 tablespoons olive oil
1 tablespoon lemon juice
1 tablespoon red wine vinegar
½ teaspoon dried oregano
2 garlic cloves, crushed
2 pinches salt + 1 turn of the
  pepper mill
3 teaspoons finely chopped red onion
3 teaspoons finely chopped bell
  pepper, preferably yellow or orange

SALAD

9 oz cherry or grape tomatoes
3 anchovies
1 small cucumber, seeded
  and diced
2 bell peppers, preferably yellow
  or orange, diced
½ red onion, diced
9 oz feta cheese, diced
3½ oz black, dry-salted olives

THE DRESSING

Whisk together the oil, lemon juice, vinegar, and oregano, then add the remaining ingredients and combine.

THE SALAD

Cut the tomatoes in half lengthways. Halve the anchovies and put them, the cucumber, bell pepper, and onion in a salad bowl. Add the feta and black olives, pour over the dressing, and mix gently so as not to crush the feta and anchovies. Refrigerate for at least 30 minutes and serve cold.

DILL POTATO SALAD

This salad is the perfect side for your meat sandwiches.

SERVES 6

Preparation time: 20 minutes
Cooking time: 10 minutes
Refrigeration time: 1 hour

SALAD

1 lb 9 oz new potatoes
1¾ oz red onion, finely chopped
1½ tablespoons capers

DRESSING

3 tablespoons superfine sugar
2 pinches salt + 2 turns of the
    pepper mill
1 garlic clove, chopped
1½ tablespoons rice vinegar
¼ cup plain mayonnaise (page 264)
¼ cup plain yogurt
1 tablespoon fresh dill, finely
chopped

THE SALAD

Peel and cut the potatoes into quarters, or smaller if the potatoes are large. Place in a pot of cold water. Bring the water and potatoes to a boil, and cook for about 10 minutes over medium heat. Test for doneness with a knife: The potato cubes should still be just a little firm. Drain and rinse with cold water.

Put the red onion in a bowl of cold water for a few minutes, then drain carefully. Place the cooled potato, red onion, and capers in a salad bowl.

THE DRESSING

Combine all of the ingredients except the dill in a large bowl.

SERVING

Combine the dressing with the mixture of potatoes and red onion. Add the dill, and stir the salad gently so as not to crush the potatoes. Refrigerate and serve chilled.

MACARONI SALAD

The many pieces of raw vegetables make all the difference.

SERVES 5

Preparation time: 20 minutes
Cooking time: 10 minutes
Refrigeration time: 30 minutes

SALAD

½ cup macaroni
olive oil
10½ oz carrot
2½ oz celery
12 small pickles, chopped

DRESSING

1⅓ cups plain mayonnaise (page 264)
3 tablespoons rice vinegar (preferably flavored
  with tarragon)
1 tablespoon superfine sugar
2 pinches salt + 2 turns of the pepper mill
1½ tablespoons Italian flat-leaf parsley, finely chopped

THE SALAD

Cook the pasta until *al dente* in a large pot of salted
water. Drain and rinse under cold water. Drizzle with
olive oil so the macaroni doesn't stick together. Peel
the carrots, trim the base and leaves of the celery
stalks, and finely chop both. Gently combine the
carrots, celery, pickles, and macaroni in a salad bowl.

THE DRESSING

Whisk the dressing ingredients together, then gently
mix into the macaroni. Refrigerate for at least
30 minutes before serving.

DILL POTATO SALAD AND COLESLAW

See recipes page 114 and page 265.

WALDORF SALAD

*This salad of apple and celery, now a classic,
was created in the late 1890s by Oscar Tschirky,
the maître d'hôtel at the Waldorf Astoria in New York.*

SERVES 1

Preparation time: 30 minutes
Cooking time: 10 minutes

SALAD

¼ cup water
¼ cup superfine sugar
1¼ cups whole pecans
7 oz celeriac
2 granny smith apples (about
    10½ oz), cored, not peeled

DRESSING

⅓ cup lemon mayonnaise (page 264)
⅓ cup plain yogurt
1 teaspoon honey
1 pinch salt + 1 turn of the
    pepper mill
2 teaspoons snipped fresh chives

THE SALAD

Place the water, sugar, and pecans in a saucepan, bring to a simmer over medium heat, and cook for about 8–10 minutes. The syrup takes on a light color, and when the pecans are well coated, empty the contents of the saucepan onto a wire rack placed over a tray. Separate the pecans with a spatula so you don't burn yourself. Allow to cool. Cut the celeriac and apples into matchsticks using a knife or a food processor. Place them in a bowl of cold water.

THE DRESSING

Combine all of the ingredients except the chives in a salad bowl.

ASSEMBLING AND SERVING

Drain the celeriac and apples and dry them well with paper towels or a clean dish towel. Combine them with the dressing.
Add the chives and refrigerate.
At serving time, add the caramelized pecans.

CAESAR SALAD

A lot of restaurants used to make a big show of preparing this salad in front of customers at the table. Today, table-prepared Caesar salads are rare, but a fresh homemade dressing is still a must.

SERVES 1
Preparation time: 20 minutes

DRESSING
1 egg yolk

3 teaspoons lemon juice

1 teaspoon Dijon mustard

6 tablespoons sunflower or canola oil

1 teaspoon anchovy paste (or the same amount of crushed anchovies), or Worcestershire sauce

½ teaspoon light honey

3 garlic cloves, crushed

2 tablespoons shredded Parmesan cheese, plus extra to serve

SALAD
12 leaves of romaine lettuce

6 large croutons (page 264)

3 teaspoons capers

THE DRESSING
All of the ingredients should be at room temperature to facilitate the emulsion. In a deep bowl, whisk the egg yolk, lemon juice, and mustard until well blended. Pour in the oil very slowly while continuing to whisk. Once you have a nice emulsion, add the rest of the dressing ingredients and mix until combined.

THE SALAD
Wash, dry, and cut the lettuce. Gently combine the lettuce with the dressing then transfer the dressed lettuce to a serving platter or bowl. Top with the croutons, capers, and extra Parmesan.

tip: Make your own anchovy paste by crushing whole anchovies with a fork. Process them with the sauce until perfectly smooth.

BLT (BACON, LETTUCE & TOMATO)

This simple bacon sandwich can be as great or mediocre as the ingredients you choose to use. Putting it together is utterly simple.

MAKES 1 SANDWICH

Preparation time: 10 minutes
Cooking time: 10 minutes

INGREDIENTS

3 or 4 slices of smoked bacon
2 slices bread
1 tablespoon sweet/unsalted butter
1½ tablespoons mayonnaise
   (page 264)
2 or 3 lettuce leaves
2 or 3 slices of tomato

THE BREAD

Brown the bacon in a frying pan (see page 88). While the bacon is cooking, toast and butter the slices of bread, then spread them with mayonnaise. Season with salt and pepper.

THE FILLING

Stack the lettuce, tomato, and bacon on one of the two bread slices and top the sandwich with the other slice.

You can poke a toothpick into the sandwich to help it hold together better, then cut it in half.

tip: Timing is important. Ideally, you want the toast and bacon to still be warm when you serve the sandwich. A BLT that has been sitting around should still be enjoyable to eat, but not quite as over-the-top as a fresh hot one.

GRILLED CHEESE SANDWICH

With such a simple dish as a grilled cheese sandwich, having high-quality ingredients will obviously be key.

MAKES 1 SANDWICH

Preparation time: 5 minutes
Cooking time: about 5 minutes

INGREDIENTS

2 slices sandwich bread
sweet/unsalted butter, softened
2 cheese slices (cheddar
   is the most traditional choice,
   but any good cheese, such as
   Gruyère or Swiss, will work well)

Heat a frying pan over medium–low heat. Generously smear butter on one side of one of the slices of bread and place the slice, buttered side down, in the frying pan. Lay the sliced cheese on top. Generously butter the other slice of bread and place it on top of the cheese slice in the pan, buttered side up.

After a couple of minutes, when the bottom slice is nicely browned, slide a wide spatula underneath and, holding the sandwich together with your free hand, turn it over. Continue cooking until the second side is golden brown and the cheese starts oozing out the sides. If your bread is looking browned before the cheese starts to ooze, the heat is too high.

note: *There are endless variations on the basic grilled cheese sandwich. In addition to mixing up different types of bread and cheese, some common additions to the sandwich include mayonnaise, ham, tomato, and tuna salad. With tuna salad, it's called a "tuna melt" (see recipe page 126).*

TUNA MELT

A grilled cheese sandwich with a tuna salad filling.
This is my tuna salad recipe.

MAKES 2 CLUB SANDWICHES

Preparation time: 15 minutes
Cooking time: 10–12 minutes

TUNA SALAD

7 oz canned tuna (drained)
2 tablespoons olive oil
2 teaspoons lemon juice
3 teaspoons light honey
2 teaspoons Dijon mustard
2½ oz celery, finely chopped
1 tablespoon finely chopped onion
¼ cup mayonnaise
salt and pepper

SANDWICHES

¼ cup sweet/unsalted butter
6 slices sandwich bread
8 cheese slices (such as
    sharp cheddar)

THE TUNA SALAD

Mix all of the ingredients together with a fork until well combined. Drain the salad in a large colander to remove excess liquid.

ASSEMBLY

Butter the slices of bread. Pan-fry one of the slices, buttered side down, with a slice of cheese on top. Set the slice aside: This will be the middle slice of the sandwich.

On a second slice of bread, place another slice of cheese on the unbuttered side, then some tuna salad, and more cheese. Top with the already browned slice, then add some tuna salad, a slice of cheese, and the last slice of bread, buttered side out.

Pan-fry the sandwich for 3–4 minutes on each side over very low heat.

Cut the sandwich on the diagonal, then proceed in the same way for the second sandwich.

FRENCH FRIES

See recipe page 128.

FRENCH FRIES

The two stages of deep-frying are the key to making perfect fries.

SERVES 6

Preparation time: 10 minutes
Resting time: 1 hour
Cooking time: 5 minutes

INGREDIENTS

2 lb 4 oz russet potatoes (allow
    about 4¼ oz per serving)
oil suitable for frying, such as
    grapeseed oil

CUTTING

Peel the potatoes using a mandolin, knife, or another tool of your choice,
then cut into long and uniform pieces.
Soak them in cold water for 1 hour to remove the surface starch which will
keep the fries from darkening too much during cooking. Drain and pat the
potatoes dry.

FRYING

In a deep-fryer or large saucepan, heat the oil until it reaches 315°F. Fry the
potatoes for 2–3 minutes until they start to bend but are still quite pale.
Drain and allow to cool at room temperature.
Increase the temperature of the oil to 375°F and fry the potatoes again for
2–3 more minutes until they're nicely browned. Undercooked fries will be
too soft, because not enough water has evaporated. Overcooked fries will
be too greasy because they will have absorbed too much oil. Perfectly cooked
fries take practice.

SERVING

Drain the fries on paper towels. If you're not serving them immediately,
or if you're cooking them in batches, keep them warm in a preheated
200°F oven. Season with salt before serving.

LATKES

Crispy on the outside, soft in the middle, these Ashkenazi potato flapjacks are yet another delicious addition to New York's glorious tradition of fried potato.

MAKES 12 LATKES

Preparation time: 20 minutes
Cooking time: 40 minutes

INGREDIENTS

2 lb 4 oz russet potatoes
1½ tablespoons salt
cooking oil (enough for a depth
   of ⅝ inch in the cooking pan)
1 large onion, finely chopped
3 eggs, lightly whisked
1¾ oz matzo meal or potato starch
   (extra if necessary)
apple sauce and/or sour cream,
   to serve

THE POTATOES

Peel and shred half the potatoes (1 lb 2 oz), mix in the salt, cover with cold water, and set aside while you prepare the boiled potatoes.
Peel the other half of the potatoes and cut them into small pieces. Place them in a pot of cold water. Bring to a boil, then lower the heat to a simmer, and cook for about 15 minutes until the potatoes are tender. Drain them, allow to cool, and mash them with a fork or potato masher.

COOKING THE LATKES

Heat the oil in a deep frying pan over medium heat. Squeeze as much water as possible out of the shredded potatoes and add them to the mashed potatoes, along with the onion and eggs. Add the matzo meal or potato starch to thicken the mixture so that the patties aren't overly wet when you put them in the oil. Test the oil with a little potato mixture—it should be just hot enough to sizzle, but not so hot that it burns right away.
Shape the mixture into 12 patties between the palms of your hands and place half of them in the oil. After a minute of frying, flatten the patties a little with the back of a spatula. After about 5 minutes, turn them over, and continue cooking on the other side for another 5 minutes or so. If the underside of the latkes is cooking too slowly or too quickly, adjust the heat accordingly. Season with salt and pepper and repeat with the remaining patties.

SERVING

Drain the latkes on paper towels. If you're not serving them immediately, or if you're cooking them in batches, keep the latkes warm in a preheated 200°F oven. Serve with apple sauce and/or sour cream.

note: Feel free to replace the potatoes with other root vegetables such as sweet potato.

1. 2 EGGS ANY STYLE 4 4 0

5. PANCAKES OR
FRENCH TOAST 4 6 0

2. ABOVE PLUS BACON
HAM, SAUSAGE OR
CORNED BEEF HASH 5 1 0

CHALLAH BREAO
FRENCH TOAST 5 6 5

5 6 5

2.30

40 EXTRA

.5 EXTRA

.55 EXTRA

PIEROGI

*Pierogi, sautéed potato ravioli, are one of the things
I love to eat in Polish or Ukrainian restaurants, such
as the Stage Restaurant on Manhattan's Lower East Side.*

MAKES 25 PIEROGI

Preparation time: 1 hour
Resting time: 1 hour
Cooking time: 50–55 minutes

PASTA DOUGH (FOR 50 PIEROGI)

3⅓ cups all-purpose flour
1 teaspoon salt
3 teaspoons sunflower oil
1 egg
1 cup water

FILLING (FOR 25 PIEROGI)

13 oz potatoes
1 onion, finely chopped
1½ tablespoons cooking oil

TOPPING

2 onions, roughly chopped
¼ cup cooking oil
sour cream or apple sauce, to serve

THE PASTA DOUGH

Process all of the ingredients together and knead until the dough
is very elastic (5–10 minutes in an electric mixer, 10–20 minutes
by hand). Form a smooth ball of dough. Place the dough in an oiled
container, cover with plastic wrap, and let it rest for 1 hour at room
temperature. Divide into two portions so that each is large enough
to make 25 pierogi. The unused portion of dough can be wrapped
in plastic wrap and frozen.

THE FILLING

Peel and cut the potatoes into small pieces of about the same size.
Place in a pot of cold water. Bring to a boil, then lower the heat and
simmer for about 15 minutes until the potatoes are tender. Drain.
Meanwhile, sauté the chopped onion in the oil over medium heat
for 5–10 minutes until softened and slightly brown. Mash the
potatoes and onion into the oil with a fork. Season with salt
and pepper.

SHAPING AND COOKING

Divide a portion of dough into 25 balls and roll them out into rounds
⅛ inch thick. Shape balls of filling using a tablespoon and place each
ball on a round of pasta. Fold the pasta dough over and press the
edges with a fork to seal well (see illustration).
Cook the pierogi in a large pot of boiling water for about 5 minutes.
Pour a little oil into the water and stir to keep the pierogi from
sticking together. Drain, then fry the pierogi in about ½ inch
of butter or cooking oil until they are crisp and golden brown
on all sides.

THE TOPPING

Sauté the onions in the oil over low heat, stirring occasionally, for
about 20 minutes until they are translucent. Continue cooking
over medium heat, continuing to stir, for another 5–10 minutes
until they're well browned but not burnt. Scatter them over the hot
sautéed pierogi and serve with sour cream or apple sauce on the side.

CHINATOWN

A neighborhood that expresses a world of its own: Traditional Chinese restaurants serving Sichuan and Cantonese food, Vietnamese and Malaysian restaurants, Peking duck restaurants, fish markets, coffee shops, dim sum, bubble tea cafés, ice cream shops, and more …

34 沾記酒家

PORK BUNS

In a typical New York mixed marriage, this popular Chinatown fast food can be recreated at home by combining the basic challah dough recipe with a not-particularly-kosher pork shoulder, marinated in a homemade char siu sauce, with no MSG or food coloring.

MAKES 15 BUNS

Preparation time: 15 minutes
Marinating time: 12–24 hours
Cooking time: 1–1 hour 15 minutes
Resting time: 1 hour

CHAR SIU MARINADE

1 oz peanut butter (page 263)
½ cup soy sauce
8 oz light honey, golden syrup or
    corn syrup
2 garlic cloves, crushed
2 teaspoons rice vinegar
3 tablespoons rice vinegar or
    Mei Kuei Lu Chiew
    (Chinese rose wine)
1½ teaspoons Chinese five-spice
2 pinches baking soda

INGREDIENTS

1 lb 10 oz pork shoulder or loin
2 pinches cornstarch
1 quantity challah dough (page 14)

THE MARINADE

In a bowl, make a slurry by combining the peanut butter with the same amount of soy sauce. Gradually add the rest of the soy sauce. Mix in the rest of the char siu marinade ingredients, finishing with the baking soda. For a saucier bun, set aside 2–3 tablespoons of sauce before adding the baking soda. You can dress the pork with this sauce after it has been baked and chopped, and before it is wrapped in the dough.

THE MEAT

Trim any excess fat from the pork and make a series of deep incisions at ¾ inch intervals. Cover the pork with the marinade inside a zippered storage bag. Close the bag, removing as much air as possible, and place it in the refrigerator. The pork should be completely submerged in the sauce. Marinate for 12–24 hours.
Preheat the oven to 450°F. Cook the meat on a wire rack in a roasting pan for 45–55 minutes until the internal temperature reaches a minimum of 144°F. Allow the meat to cool and chop into small pieces. Toss the meat in the cornstarch, then, if you put aside any char siu sauce without the baking soda, add it to the meat as well.

SHAPING AND COOKING

Make the challah dough following the recipe on page 14 to the first rise. Divide the dough into 15 equal portions.
Make a hollow in the middle of each portion of dough, place about 1½ oz roast pork into the hollow and pinch the dough closed around the meat. Place the closed buns on a baking sheet lined with parchment paper. Dust with flour and cover loosely with plastic wrap. Let the buns rise for 1 hour at room temperature.
Preheat the oven to 350°F. Brush the tops of the buns with the egg white and sugar glaze from the challah recipe. Cook the buns for 15–20 minutes until golden brown.

SESAME NOODLES

When I was a kid I always ordered these sweet and tangy noodles from the local Chinese take-out.

SERVES 3

Preparation time: 20 minutes
Cooking time: varies depending
    on the type of noodles

INGREDIENTS

1 lb 12 oz fresh Chinese egg noodles
    (or 14 oz if they are dried)
3½ oz sliced cucumbers or pickles,
    to serve
1–2 tablespoons toasted black or
    white sesame seeds, to serve

SAUCE

4 garlic cloves
1 tablespoon peeled and finely
    chopped fresh ginger
1–2 tablespoons sugar (according
    to taste)
½ cup water
1¾ oz Chinese sesame paste
3 tablespoons sesame oil
¼ cup peanut butter (page 263)
1 tablespoon rice vinegar
1½ tablespoons soy sauce

THE NOODLES

Cook the noodles according to the directions on the package. Once cooked, drain, and plunge the noodles into iced water.

THE SAUCE

Crush the garlic with a garlic press or chop it finely using a knife. Both garlic and ginger can then be ground in a mortar and pestle with the sugar or blended with the water in a blender or food processor. The aim is to grind up the garlic and ginger as finely as possible.

Mix in the rest of the sauce ingredients with a whisk or fork until well combined.

Pour the sauce over the noodles gradually until they're as saucy as you like them, tossing them gently with your fingers or a chopstick.

SERVING

Serve cold with slices of cucumber or pickle, and a sprinkling of toasted sesame seeds.

SPICED PINEAPPLE

See "fast pickles" recipes page 242.

tip: If you have raw sesame seeds, you can spread them out in one layer in a frying pan over medium heat and toast them, shaking the pan from time to time, for about 3 minutes until they're evenly browned.

CLAYPOT SALMON AND SALAD

*My colleague Ngan Tran, who grew up in Vietnamese restaurants
in the south of France, was kind enough to share her family's
recipes for two favorite dishes I used to eat in Chinatown.*

CLAYPOT SALMON
SERVES 4

Preparation time: 15 minutes
Resting time: 2 hours to overnight
Cooking time: 25 minutes

INGREDIENTS

4 salmon steaks
6 tablespoons fish sauce
3 tablespoons mushroom flavored
    dark soy sauce
1½ tablespoons sugar
2 garlic cloves, crushed
4 large pieces of fresh pineapple
cilantro leaves, to serve

GREEN PAPAYA SALAD
SERVES 4

Preparation time: 15 minutes
Cooking time: 5 minutes

INGREDIENTS

1 green papaya, peeled and shredded
2 carrots, shredded
½ bunch mint, coarsely chopped
½ bunch cilantro, coarsely chopped
3 tablespoons sunflower oil
2 garlic cloves, chopped
1½ limes, juiced
⅓ cup fish sauce
3 teaspoons dark brown sugar
1 teaspoon salt
1 chili, chopped (optional)
fresh ginger, chopped, to taste
2 tablespoons toasted peanuts,
    chopped

CLAYPOT SALMON

THE MARINADE

Make the marinade the night before, or at least 2 hours before
cooking. Place the steaks in a mixing bowl and pour over
3 tablespoons fish sauce, 1 tablespoon mushroom dark soy sauce,
half the sugar, and 1 crushed garlic clove. Combine gently, cover
with plastic wrap, and set aside. Refrigerate if resting overnight.

COOKING

Drizzle some oil in a flameproof casserole dish or heavy saucepan and
lay the drained salmon steaks, pineapple, and the remaining crushed
garlic clove on top. Add the remaining fish sauce, mushroom dark
soy sauce, sugar, and some salt. Cover with water and bring to a boil.
Adjust the seasoning (the sauce should be both sweet and salty), then
carefully turn the steaks over. Cook at a gentle simmer on a low heat,
covered, for 20–25 minutes. The sauce should reduce to just a
caramelized layer in the bottom of the pan; if this is not the case,
uncover, and continue to reduce for a few minutes.

SERVING

Garnish with cilantro, season generously with pepper, and serve with
white rice, and a salad or soup.

GREEN PAPAYA SALAD

THE SALAD

Combine the green papaya, carrots, mint, and cilantro.

THE DRESSING

In a small saucepan, heat the oil over low heat and fry the chopped
garlic. Once browned, allow to cool in the oil. Make the sauce by
combining the lime juice, fish sauce, sugar, salt, and chopped chili. Add
the toasted garlic and oil, and the ginger. Pour the dressing over the
salad just before serving. Gently toss and sprinkle with the peanuts.

ROAST CHICKEN

To achieve a roast chicken at home with skin as crispy and meat as flavorful as the ones from the rotisseries on Manhattan's Upper West Side, I employ two techniques: I marinate the chicken in a saltwater brine; and I cook it slowly on a rack.

FOR A 3 LB 5 OZ–4 LB 8 OZ CHICKEN

Preparation time: 15 minutes
Resting time: at least 5 hours
Cooking time: 2½–3 hours

BRINE

14 cups water
1 lb 2 oz non-iodized salt
1⅓ cups sugar
2 teaspoons black or yellow
    mustard seeds
1 teaspoon black peppercorns
2 lemons, quartered

RUB

¼ cup butter or olive oil
2 tablespoons light honey or maple
    syrup (optional)
1–2 teaspoons cayenne pepper
1–2 teaspoons ground cumin
2 teaspoons salt
3 pinches ground black pepper

BRINING AND DRYING

Combine all of the brining ingredients together, except for the quartered lemons, in a large pot, and stir over high heat until the sugar and salt have dissolved.

Allow to cool at room temperature. As it takes a while for the brine to cool down, do this the day before or replace 2 cups water with ice, which you can add once everything is dissolved, to quickly lower the temperature.

In a large pot or bucket, submerge the chicken in the cooled brine with the quartered lemons. Cover and refrigerate for at least 2 hours per 2 lb 4 oz, but not for more than 12 hours. Rinse, pat dry with kitchen paper, and let it rest again in the refrigerator on a wire rack, uncovered, for 2–12 hours—air-drying the chicken in this way will help make the chicken more crispy.

RUBBING AND COOKING

Preheat the oven to 235°F. Whisk all of the rub ingredients together and spread over the whole of the chicken and inside the cavity. Place the chicken on its back on a V-shaped roasting rack (see photo). Cook for 1½ hours. Turn the chicken over and return to the oven for another 1–1½ hours until the juices run clear when you pierce the chicken with a knife or skewer, or until a meat thermometer inserted into the deepest part of the thigh reads at least 165°F.

MATZO BALL SOUP

The matzo balls are really the star attraction in this soup, but you can make it without them, in which case it would just be a classic chicken soup (aka "Jewish penicillin.")

SERVES 5

Preparation time: 30 minutes
Refrigeration time: 3 hours
Cooking time: 45 minutes

BALLS

5½ oz matzo meal
2 pinches baking soda
1 teaspoon ground cinnamon
    (optional)
4 eggs, separated
¼ cup olive oil
¼ cup water
1 teaspoon parsley, finely chopped
½ teaspoon salt

BASE

1 carrot, diced
1 parsnip, diced
1 onion, finely chopped
4 garlic cloves, crushed
1 teaspoon dried thyme
2 tablespoons olive oil
8 cups chicken stock (page 265)
3½ oz dried egg noodles
12 small pieces of cooked chicken
    (e.g. chicken leftovers, see
    previous page)

THE BALLS

Mix together the matzo meal, baking soda, and cinnamon. Beat together the egg yolks, oil, water, and parsley. Combine the two mixtures.

Beat the egg whites with the salt until stiff peaks form. Gently fold the beaten egg whites into the rest and refrigerate for at least 3 hours. With oiled hands, roll the matzo ball dough into balls the size of a table tennis ball.

THE BASE

Sauté the vegetables, garlic, and thyme in the olive oil over medium heat for about 5 minutes until the onion is translucent, then add the chicken stock. Bring to the boil, then lower the heat to a simmer. Season with salt and pepper. Add the matzo balls 30 minutes before serving, the dried egg noodles 10 minutes before serving, and the pieces of chicken 5 minutes before serving. To reduce the total cooking time, the matzo balls can also be pre-cooked separately in salted water and then added to the soup with the chicken just before serving.

MUSHROOM BARLEY SOUP

Super tender slow-cooked beef cheek or brisket is the key to this rustic winter classic.

SERVES 8

Preparation time: 30 minutes
Cooking time: about 4 hours

STOCK AND MEAT

1 onion, roughly chopped
1½ tablespoons olive oil
⅓ cup roughly chopped celery
⅓ cup roughly chopped carrot
9 oz beef cheeks or brisket, cut into
    large cubes
4 garlic cloves
¼ cup white wine
2 teaspoons salt
12 cups water

OTHER INGREDIENTS

1 cup pearl barley
1 lb 2 oz mushrooms, thinly sliced
3 tablespoons olive oil
1 onion, chopped
1½ cups combination of celery,
    carrot, and parsnip, diced
2 bay leaves
1 large sprig thyme
3 tablespoons white wine
¼ cup cornstarch (adjust according
    to the consistency)
parsley, to serve

THE STOCK AND THE MEAT

In a soup pot, sauté the onion in the olive oil over medium heat until translucent. Add the celery and carrot, and cook for another 5 minutes. Add the meat and continue cooking for 5 minutes, stirring until browned on all sides. Add the garlic and continue to cook for a couple of minutes. Add the white wine and cook for a few minutes, then add the salt and water. Bring to a boil, then reduce the heat and simmer over low heat for 2½ hours, skimming and discarding any scum that rises to the surface. Remove the meat and set aside to add back to the soup later. Strain the rest through a colander over a bowl or large pot and discard the solids. You should have a little more than 8 cups of stock, which you can set aside. If the stock has reduced to less than this, you can extend it by adding more water.

THE SOUP

Rinse the barley and cook in boiling water (at least three times the volume of the barley) for about 30 minutes until tender. Drain the barley and set aside.

Cut the meat into small pieces and set aside. It should be super tender at this point and will more or less disintegrate into small strands when it goes back into the soup.

In a soup pot, sauté the mushrooms in the olive oil over high heat for a few minutes, then add the onion, celery, carrot, parsnip, bay leaves, and thyme, and lower the heat to medium. Cook for 5 more minutes, stirring. Add the reserved stock, bring to a boil, then lower the heat to a simmer. Cook for about 20 minutes or until the vegetables are tender. Blend the white wine with the cornstarch, mix it into the soup, and simmer until slightly thickened. Season with salt and pepper.

SERVING

Add the meat and barley to the simmering soup 5 minutes before serving. Serve garnished with some chopped parsley.

SPLIT PEA SOUP

On a cold winter's day, a hot bowl of smooth split pea soup with a few croutons thrown in hits the spot like nothing else.

SERVES 5

Preparation time: 30 minutes
Soaking time: overnight
Cooking time: 1 hour 45 minutes

INGREDIENTS

2¼ cups split green peas
¼ cup olive oil
1 onion, roughly chopped
¾ cup roughly chopped carrots
⅓ cup roughly chopped celery
3 garlic cloves, chopped
1 teaspoon smoked paprika
1 teaspoon ground cumin
1 bunch cilantro, stems
   and leaves separated
6 cups water
2 teaspoons cider vinegar
3 teaspoons sugar
1 teaspoon salt
½ teaspoon ground black pepper

GARNISH

⅓ cup yogurt or sour cream
   (optional)
about 20 croutons (page 264)

THE SPLIT PEAS

Soak the split peas in cold water overnight. Discard the water and rinse. While many recipes indicate that it is not necessary to soak split peas, I find that presoaking them produces a less starchy, more digestible soup that is also easier to make since it cooks faster and doesn't stick as much to the bottom of the pot. You could, however, skip this step, but you should at least rinse the split peas.

COOKING

Heat 1½ tablespoons of the olive oil in a soup pot over medium heat. Sauté the onion, carrot, celery, and garlic and cook for about 5 minutes. Add the spices and chopped cilantro stems, and cook for another 5 minutes, stirring regularly.

Add the rinsed peas and cover them with about three-quarters of the water. Bring to a boil and then lower the heat. Simmer for 1½ hours or more, until the peas are soft and naturally disintegrate into a purée. Skim and discard any scum that rises to the top as you go. Check regularly to make sure that the peas are not sticking to the bottom of the pot; if they start to stick, turn off the heat. After a few minutes, the stuck (but hopefully not burnt) layer should come away easily with a spatula and you can then resume simmering the soup.

Blend the soup with an immersion blender until smooth. Add as much of the remaining water as needed, and more if necessary, to achieve the desired consistency. Add the vinegar, remaining oil, sugar, salt, and pepper.

THE GARNISH

Ladle the soup into bowls. Finely chop the cilantro leaves, then scatter them over the soup. Drop 1 tablespoon of yogurt or sour cream in each bowl, then add a few croutons.

CORN BREAD

See recipe page 150.

CORNBREAD

*Cornbread is usually enjoyed with savory food, but it is also delicious
on its own with a little butter and jam, or honey.*

MAKES 16 PIECES
Preparation time: 10 minutes
Cooking time: about 45 minutes

DRY INGREDIENTS
1⅓ cups all-purpose flour
1 cup fine cornmeal
1½ teaspoons baking powder
2 pinches baking soda
½ teaspoon salt

WET INGREDIENTS
1¾ cups buttermilk
5 tablespoons sweet/unsalted
    butter, melted
2 eggs
1 cup cooked corn kernels
    off the cob
⅓ small green chili, finely chopped
    (optional)

THE BATTER
Preheat the oven to 375°F. Butter a 9 x 9 x 1½ inch square cake pan and
sprinkle with sugar.
Combine all the dry ingredients together, then beat together the wet
ingredients. Combine the two mixtures without overworking the batter.

COOKING
Pour the batter into the pan and bake for about 45 minutes until a skewer
inserted into the middle comes out clean.

MAC & CHEESE

Feed the kids (or your inner child). Nobody is ever disappointed with this gratin of macaroni with a cheese sauce.

SERVES 5
Preparation time: 20 minutes
Cooking time: about 50 minutes

INGREDIENTS
1 lb 2 oz macaroni

CHEESE SAUCE
1¾ oz butter
1½ tablespoons all-purpose flour
1¾ cups evaporated milk
1 teaspoon Dijon mustard
2 teaspoons salt
1¼ cups milk
3 cups shredded cheddar cheese
    (or similar cheese, such as Colby
    or Monterey Jack)

GRATIN
2⅔ cups day old breadcrumbs
3 tablespoons sweet/unsalted
    butter, melted

THE PASTA
Cook the macaroni in salted water according to the directions on the package until *al dente*. Drain and rinse with cold water to keep it from cooking further.

THE CHEESE SAUCE
Heat the butter in a saucepan over medium heat. After a few minutes, when bubbles start to form, add the flour. Stir constantly while cooking the mixture until it starts to turn a light brown. Slowly add the evaporated milk while continuing to stir. Mix in the mustard and salt. Continue stirring and cooking for another few minutes until smooth and thick. Add the milk and cheese, and stir until the cheese is melted. Turn off the heat and add the cooked macaroni to the sauce.

THE GRATIN
Preheat the oven to 350°F. Transfer the macaroni and cheese to an appropriately sized baking dish. It's normal for the mixture to seem quite liquid, but it will thicken during cooking. Combine the breadcrumbs and melted butter and sprinkle over the top. Bake for 30 minutes.

tip: For a cheesier version, reduce the quantity of macaroni by 20–25%.

NOODLE KUGLE
See recipe page 154.

NOODLE KUGEL

In my family, we like to have warm noodle pudding with roast chicken, but it is also great cold on its own the next day.

SERVES 10

Preparation time: 20 minutes
Cooking time: about 1 hour

BASE

9 oz dried egg noodles
6 eggs, beaten
3 tablespoons sunflower oil
11½ oz apple sauce
½ cup light brown sugar (or ⅓ cup
    sugar + 1 teaspoon molasses)
½ cup golden raisins
3 teaspoons ground cinnamon
½ teaspoon salt

TOPPING

5½ oz granny smith apple, diced
3 teaspoons demerara sugar

THE NOODLES

Preheat the oven to 350°F. Cook the noodles in boiling salted water according to the directions on the package until they're *al dente*. Drain.

THE BASE AND COOKING

Combine all of the base ingredients together, including the drained noodles, and transfer the mixture to a large baking dish lined with parchment paper. Spread the diced apple over the noodles and sprinkle the sugar over the top. Cover with foil and bake for about 45 minutes. Remove the sheet of foil 10 minutes before the end of cooking.

SLOPPY JOES

A kids' favorite, Sloppy Joes can be, as its name suggests, a messy experience. All the better!

MAKES 6 SANDWICHES

Preparation time: 25 minutes
Cooking time: about 1 hour

INGREDIENTS

1 lb 2 oz lean ground meat such as sirloin
1 onion, finely chopped
3 garlic cloves, crushed
1 green bell pepper, seeded and diced
1½ cups puréed tomatoes
¼ cup ketchup (page 264)
1 teaspoon Worcestershire sauce
3 teaspoons light brown sugar
1 teaspoon mustard
½ cup water
1 teaspoon salt & 1 pinch black pepper
3 drops hot pepper sauce
6 hot dog buns (page 102)

THE MEAT

Heat a frying pan over medium heat. Add the ground meat and onion to the pan and cook for 10 minutes, breaking up the lumps with a spatula. The meat should be well browned and crumbly. Add the garlic and bell pepper and cook for 3 more minutes.
Add the tomato purée, ketchup, Worcestershire sauce, sugar, and mustard. Then add the water, salt, pepper, and hot pepper sauce. When the sauce starts to boil, reduce the heat as low as possible, and simmer for about 40 minutes, stirring regularly.

THE SANDWICH

Serve hot in a hot dog (or hamburger) bun.

THE ONION RINGS

See recipe page 265.

KNISH

These stuffed buns were brought to New York by immigrants from Eastern Europe in the early 1900s.

MAKES 7 KNISHES

Preparation time: 40 minutes
Cooking time: 1 hour 10 minutes

FILLING

11¼ oz potatoes, cut into cubes
1 onion, finely chopped
1½ tablespoons cooking oil
3 teaspoons matzo meal or ordinary
    breadcrumbs
3 pinches sugar
1 egg, beaten (set 2 teaspoons aside
    for glazing)

DOUGH

1¼ cups all-purpose flour
1 teaspoon baking powder
1½ tablespoons sunflower oil
1 egg
3 tablespoons water
2 pinches salt

THE FILLING

Place the potatoes in a large pot of cold water, bring to a boil, then lower the heat and simmer for 20 minutes until they are quite tender. Drain. Meanwhile, sauté the onion in the oil over medium heat for 5–10 minutes until softened and lightly brown. Mash the potatoes and onion with the oil using a fork, and incorporate the breadcrumbs, sugar, and beaten egg. Season with salt and pepper.

THE DOUGH

Using a food processor or by hand, mix until until combined.

SHAPING AND COOKING

Preheat the oven to 350°F. On a floured surface, roll out the dough into a rectangular shape about 11¼ inches long and ¼ inch thick. Spread the filling in a sausage shape along the length of the rectangle, then roll the dough over the sausage and pinch the ends of the tube to close it.

With the side of your hand or a chopstick, make six dents along the length of the sausage. Separate the portions using a knife or dough cutter. You obtain seven sections that are open on both sides. Pinch one end closed and reshape the knish so it's round (it will have been put out of shape by the cutting). Pinch the sides at the other end towards the center, leaving a small opening (this is the top of the knish). Place the shaped knishes on a baking sheet lined with parchment paper. Brush the tops with the reserved egg and bake for about 40 minutes until golden brown.

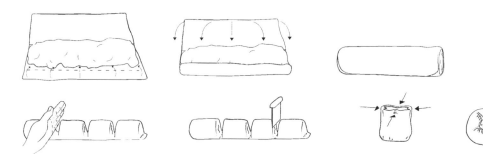

STUFFED CABBAGE

My grandmother, Minnie Grossman, made this amazing sweet-and-sour stuffed cabbage. She showed me how to make it once, but nothing was written down and for years I've been trying to figure out the recipe. This is not far off.

SERVES 5–6

Preparation time: 30 minutes
Cooking time: 1 hour 45 minutes

INGREDIENTS

1 green cabbage

STUFFING

9 oz ground beef
9 oz ground veal
¼ cup jasmine rice
½ teaspoon salt
1 pinch ground black pepper
1 egg, beaten

SAUCE

¾ cup puréed tomatoes
¾ cup cranberry juice
½ cup (lightly packed) light
   brown sugar
3½ oz dried fruit (figs,
   golden raisins …)

THE CABBAGE

Boil the cabbage whole in a large pot of water for about 15 minutes until the leaves are pliable. Drain and allow to cool. Remove 10–12 large leaves to use for the cabbage rolls. Trim down the thick ribs at the base of the cabbage leaves so they can be rolled without breaking.

STUFFING AND FOLDING

Preheat the oven to 350°F. Mix all of the stuffing ingredients together and divide into 10–12 portions. Place each portion of meat at the bottom of a cabbage leaf and roll the leaf to enclose it, folding in the sides.

COOKING AND SERVING

Place the rolls, seam side down, in a deep roasting dish. Use some of the leftover cabbage to fill any gaps so that the rolls are packed in tight. Combine all of the sauce ingredients and pour it over the rolls. Cover the dish with foil and cook for 1½ hours.
Leftovers can be frozen and reheated in a frying pan with a little water. For some reason, I always had the impression my grandmother's stuffed cabbage was even better thawed and reheated than it was fresh.

KNISHES

See recipe page 158.

MEATLOAF & GRAVY

An American diner classic.

SERVES 6

Preparation time: 30 minutes
Cooking time: 1 hour 15 minutes

LOAF

½ cup finely chopped celery
½ cup finely chopped onion,
¾ cup thinly sliced mushrooms
1½ tablespoons cooking oil
12 oz ground beef
12 oz ground veal
3 tablespoons dry breadcrumbs
½ cup ketchup (page 264)
    + 3 tablespoons, to brush
    over the loaf
2 teaspoons hot pepper sauce
    (optional)
1 egg, beaten
1½ tablespoons chopped Italian
    flat-leaf parsley
2 pinches salt +1 pinch ground
    black pepper

MASHED POTATOES

2 lb 4 oz Idaho potatoes
2½ oz butter
⅓ cup milk

GRAVY

1½ tablespoons finely chopped
    onion
½ cup thinly sliced mushrooms
3 tablespoons butter
1½ tablespoons all-purpose flour
1 cup beef broth

THE LOAF

Preheat the oven to 350°F. Sauté the celery, onion, and mushrooms in the oil over medium heat until they're soft. Add the rest of the loaf ingredients and mix until combined. Turn into an 8 × 4 inch loaf pan, smooth the top, spread over the extra ketchup, and cook for 1 hour.

THE MASHED POTATOES

Cut the potatoes into pieces of the same size. Place them in a pot of cold salted water. Bring to a boil and cook for about 15 minutes until the potatoes are tender. Drain.
Melt the butter in the milk in a saucepan over medium heat. Mash together the hot potatoes and the hot milk–butter mixture using a food processor, potato masher, or a fork followed by a whisk. Season with salt and pepper. Add more milk if the mash is too dry. Serve hot.

THE GRAVY

In a saucepan, sauté the onion and mushrooms with 3 teaspoons of the butter until softened. Remove from the saucepan and set aside. Heat the remaining butter in the same saucepan. After a few minutes, when the butter starts to foam, add the flour. Stir constantly until the roux turns a light brown color. Slowly pour in the beef broth, stirring constantly. When the mixture is smooth, increase the heat and bring to a boil. Add the mushrooms and onion, and continue to cook, stirring, until it has the right consistency.

tip: *The beef broth can be replaced by a bouillon cube dissolved in 1 cup of boiling water.*

CORNED BEEF

Making a good corned beef brisket like the one in the famous
Katz sandwiches is easy, but it does take time.

MAKES ABOUT 6 SERVINGS

Preparation time: 15 minutes
Resting time: 5 days to 3 weeks
Cooking time: 4 hours

CORNING SPICES

2 teaspoons whole allspice
2 teaspoons yellow or brown mustard
    seeds, toasted and crushed
2 teaspoons dried red chili flakes
2 teaspoons whole cloves
2 teaspoons mixed peppercorns,
    toasted and crushed
2 teaspoons cardamom pods, bruised
2 bay leaves
1 teaspoon ground ginger
1 cinnamon stick, broken into pieces
2 whole pieces of mace

CORNING LIQUID

6 cups distilled water
4 oz coarse non-iodized salt
1 teaspoon potassium nitrate
    (saltpeter)
2 garlic cloves

MEAT

1 lb 10 oz beef brisket

THE CORNING SPICES

Combine all the spices together. Set aside half for the cooking liquid; the other half will be used for cooking the meat.

THE CORNING LIQUID

In a large pot, bring all the corning liquid ingredients and the half portion of the corning spices to a boil. Once the salt has completely dissolved, turn off the heat and allow the liquid to cool to room temperature, then refrigerate it. This can be done the day before.

THE CORNING

Inside a large zippered storage bag, submerge the meat in the corning liquid. Squeeze as much air as possible out of the bag. Make sure that the meat is completely submerged and place the bag in a dish in the refrigerator for 5 days to 3 weeks, turning it once or twice a day, so that the meat marinates evenly.

COOKING

Rinse the meat off and place it in a flameproof casserole dish or soup pot. Add the other half of the corning spices and add water until the meat is at least 1¼ inches under the surface of the liquid. Bring the water to a boil, then reduce the heat to low. Simmer for 3–4 hours until the meat is very tender.

You can serve the corned beef immediately, but for sandwiches it is usually best to wrap and refrigerate it first before slicing.

SPAGHETTI & MEATBALLS

Nothing fancy here. Big, authentic meatballs, a generous smothering of homemade tomato sauce, a little shredded Parmesan on top, and some garlic bread. Good old-fashioned American–Italian food.

SERVES 4

Preparation time: 30 minutes
Cooking time: 1 hour

MEATBALLS

9 oz ground beef
9 oz ground pork
2 garlic cloves, crushed
1 egg, beaten
⅓ cup Parmesan cheese, shredded
¾ cup fresh breadcrumbs
1 tablespoon finely chopped Italian
   flat-leaf parsley
¼ cup milk
½ teaspoon salt
1 pinch ground black pepper

TOMATO SAUCE

2 tablespoons finely chopped onion
1 tablespoon each of finely chopped
   carrot and celery
3 tablespoons olive oil
5 garlic cloves, crushed
2 pinches dried oregano (or basil)
2 cups puréed tomatoes
¼ cup water

GARLIC BREAD

1 baguette (not too thin)
½ cup butter, softened
1½ tablespoons olive oil
3 garlic cloves, crushed
1 tablespoon finely chopped Italian
   flat-leaf parsley

OTHER INGREDIENTS

14 oz spaghetti

THE MEATBALLS

Preheat the oven to 400°F. Mix all of the ingredients together until combined and form 10–12 large meatballs with your hands. Arrange them on a baking sheet lined with parchment paper. Bake for 15 minutes.

THE TOMATO SAUCE

Meanwhile, sauté the onion, carrot, and celery in the olive oil over medium heat for about 5 minutes until the onion is translucent. Stir in the crushed garlic, and cook for another minute before adding the oregano, tomato purée, and water. Simmer for 15 minutes. Season with salt and pepper, and a pinch of light brown sugar, if you like. Add the meatballs and simmer for 15 minutes just before serving.

THE GARLIC BREAD

Preheat the oven to 350°F. Split the baguette in half lengthwise. Mix all the other ingredients into a paste. Spread this mixture on the cut sides of the bread, and place the two halves on a baking sheet with the buttered sides up. Bake for about 10 minutes until they're slightly browned. Slice and serve with the dish.

SPAGHETTI

While you're making the garlic bread, start cooking the spaghetti. Cook in boiling salted water until *al dente*, then drain and serve with the meatballs and tomato sauce. Serve garlic bread on the side.

CHOLENT

This traditional Shabbat lunchtime stew is cooked for 15 hours.
As the song goes, "Good things come to those who wait!"

SERVES 5

Preparation time: 30 minutes
Cooking time: 15 hours

INGREDIENTS

2 lb 12 oz beef short ribs
  or other stewing beef
¼ cup olive oil
1 tablespoon salt
2 onions, finely chopped
12 garlic cloves, finely chopped
2¼ oz honey
3 teaspoons smoked paprika
1 teaspoon ground black pepper
7 oz black-eyed beans, rinsed
3½ oz pearl barley
1 lb 2 oz carrots, quartered
1 lb 2 oz turnips, halved (or left
  whole if small)
6 cups cold water (enough to cover
  the meat by at least 2 inches)

THE STEW

Preheat the oven to 200°F. Cut the meat into big evenly sized chunks and brown in 2 tablespoons of the oil with 2 teaspoons of the salt in a flameproof casserole dish over high heat. Remove the browned meat, add the rest of the oil, and sauté the onions and garlic for a few minutes. Add the honey, paprika, pepper, and remaining salt. Return the meat to the pot and coat with the sauce. Add the black-eyed beans, barley, carrots, and turnips, and cover with cold water. Bring to a boil, remove the scum from the surface, and cover with a tight-fitting lid.

COOKING IN THE OVEN

Place the casserole dish in the oven and cook for 15 hours. Usually, this is done overnight. In the morning or halfway through the cooking time, make sure that the meat is still covered with water and, if necessary, add more water so that it is at least 1¼ inches above the meat.

16 : 23

SNACK TIME

PB&J (PEANUT BUTTER & JELLY)

This all-American snack will be as mediocre or as fantastic as the ingredients you use.

MAKES 1 SANDWICH
Preparation time: 2 minutes

INGREDIENTS
2 slices whole-wheat sandwich bread
peanut butter (page 263)
jam or jelly (pages 262–263)

Take two slices of sandwich bread. Spread peanut butter on one slice and jam or jelly on the other. Put them together. Cut and serve. That's all there is to it!

CHOCOLATE CHIP COOKIES
See recipe page 226.

APPLE PIE

A quintessentially American experience.

MAKES ONE 10½ INCH PIE

Preparation time: 45 minutes, plus
    2 hours cooling
Resting time: 1 hour
Cooking time: about 1 hour 10 minutes

PASTRY

1 cup cold sweet/unsalted butter, diced
3⅓ cups all-purpose flour
1 teaspoon fine salt
¼ cup confectioners' sugar
¼ cup cold water
3 teaspoons cider vinegar

FILLING

11 small granny smith apples, peeled,
    cored, and cut into small pieces
½ cup light brown sugar
3 teaspoons ground cinnamon
1 vanilla bean, split lengthways and
    seeds scraped
2¼ tablespoons cornstarch
1½ tablespoons lemon juice or
    cider vinegar
3 tablespoons sweet/unsalted butter

GLAZE

1 egg yolk
1 teaspoon water
1 tablespoon light brown sugar

THE PASTRY

Using a food processor or butter knife, cut the butter into the dry ingredients until you have a crumbly consistency. Next, incorporate the water and vinegar by hand just until you have a smooth dough. Divide into two balls of the same size, wrap them in plastic wrap, and refrigerate for at least 1 hour.

THE FILLING

Combine the apple pieces with the brown sugar, cinnamon, and vanilla bean seeds. Blend the cornstarch with the lemon juice or cider vinegar. Heat the butter in a large frying pan over medium heat. When it starts to sizzle, add the apples and cook them until they're lightly browned on all sides—you may need to do this in batches. Add the cornstarch and lemon juice mixture, and continue to cook for 5 minutes, stirring. Remove from the heat and cool.

SHAPING AND BLIND BAKING

Preheat the oven to 350°F. If the pastry dough is too hard when it comes out of the refrigerator, let it soften. Butter and flour a 10½ inch pie dish. On a floured surface, roll out the balls of dough into two rounds large enough to hang over the edge of the dish by about 2 inches.
Place one of the rounds in the dish, then roll the overhang onto itself. Prick the pastry base with a fork, cover with parchment paper and dried beans, and bake for 15 minutes. Remove the paper and beans, and return to the oven for about 5 minutes until the pastry is dry and light golden.

COOKING AND SERVING

Pour the apple filling over the baked base. Cover with the second round of pastry dough, seal the edges by pinching them together with your fingers, and make small incisions on the top to let the pie breathe. Brush the pastry with the mixture of egg yolk and water, then sprinkle with the sugar. Place in the oven and bake for about 45 minutes.
Allow the pie to cool for 2 hours before cutting. Serve warm with a scoop of ice cream (my preference) or whipped cream (page 263).

PECAN PIE

This pecan pie has a chocolate pie crust. You will not be disappointed.

MAKES ONE 10½ INCH PIE

Preparation time: 40 minutes, plus cooling
Resting time: 2 hours
Cooking time: about 1 hour 15 minutes

PASTRY

½ cup cold sweet/unsalted butter, diced
1½ cups all-purpose flour
2 scant tablespoons cocoa powder
½ teaspoon fine salt
1½ tablespoons confectioners' sugar
2 teaspoons sugar
¼ cup cold water

FILLING

2½ cups pecans
1 cup sugar syrup*
1⅔ cups light brown sugar
   (or 1½ cups superfine sugar +
   1 tablespoon molasses)
2 pinches salt
¼ cup sweet/unsalted butter
1½ teaspoons natural vanilla extract
¼ cup half and half
6 eggs

FINISHES

1 tablespoon sugar syrup*

*To make sugar syrup, combine 1 cup sugar with 1 cup water in a saucepan and stir over low heat until the sugar dissolves. Bring to a boil and remove from the heat.

THE PASTRY

Using a food processor or butter knife, cut the butter into the dry ingredients until you have a crumbly consistency. Next, incorporate the water by hand just until you have a smooth dough. Roll into a ball, wrap it in plastic wrap, and refrigerate for at least 1 hour.

THE FILLING

Spread the pecans on a baking sheet lined with parchment paper and bake them at 350°F for 10 minutes to lightly toast them. Allow them to cool for a few minutes, then crush them coarsely.
In a saucepan, heat the sugar syrup, sugar, salt, butter, and vanilla. Allow the sugar to dissolve on a low heat, then bring to a boil. Remove from the heat and add the cream. Stir and allow to cool. Add the eggs, one at a time, taking care to whisk the mixture well after adding each egg.

SHAPING AND BLIND BAKING

Preheat the oven to 350°F. If the pastry dough is too hard when it comes out of the refrigerator, let it soften. Butter and flour a 10½ inch pie dish. On a floured surface, roll out the dough to make a round large enough to hang over the edge of the dish by about 1¼ inches.
Place the round of dough in the dish, then roll the overhang onto itself and pinch with your fingers to stick the dough together. Let it rest in the refrigerator for at least 1 hour.
Prick the pastry base with a fork, cover with parchment paper and dried beans, and bake for 15 minutes. Remove the paper and beans and return to the oven for about 5 minutes until dry and light golden.

COOKING AND SERVING

Spread the pecans over the baked pastry base and pour over the filling mixture. Place the pie in the oven and bake for about 40 minutes. The filling should be set but still a little wobbly in the center.
When you take it out of the oven, brush the edge of the pastry with sugar syrup. Allow to cool before cutting. Serve with a scoop of ice cream.

CHERRY PIE

Some things in life are actually as good as they appear …

MAKES ONE 10½ INCH PIE

Preparation time: 35 minutes, plus
    4 hours cooling
Resting time: about 1 hour
Cooking time: about 1 hour 20 minutes

PASTRY

1 cup cold sweet/unsalted butter, diced
3⅓ cups all-purpose flour
⅓ cup confectioners' sugar
1 teaspoon fine salt
¼ cup cold water
3 teaspoons lemon juice

FILLING

2¼ tablespoons cornstarch
2¼ tablespoons lemon juice
2 lb sour cherries, pitted
7 oz granny smith apples, cored and diced,
    not peeled
¾ cup superfine sugar

GLAZE

1 egg yolk
a little water
light brown or turbinado sugar, for
sprinkling

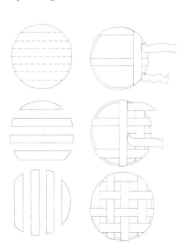

THE PASTRY

Using a food processor or butter knife, cut the butter into the dry ingredients until you have a crumbly consistency. Incorporate the water and lemon juice by hand just until you have a smooth dough. Divide into two balls of the same size, wrap them in plastic wrap, and refrigerate for at least 1 hour.

THE FILLING

Meanwhile, combine the cornstarch with the lemon juice. Place this mixture and the cherries, apple pieces, and sugar in a saucepan over medium heat. Cook for about 15 minutes, stirring. Allow to cool completely.

SHAPING AND BLIND BAKING

Preheat the oven to 350°F. If the pastry dough is too hard when it comes out of the refrigerator, let it soften. Butter and flour a 10½ inch pie dish.
On a floured surface, roll out the balls of dough into two rounds large enough to hang over the edge of the dish by about 2 inches. Place one of the rounds in the dish, then roll the overhang onto itself. Prick the pastry base with a fork, cover with parchment paper and dried beans, and bake for 15 minutes. Remove the paper and beans and return to the oven for about 5 minutes until dry and light golden. Fill the pastry shell with the cold filling. It is essential for the filling to be cold before attempting the lattice, otherwise the heat will make the strips of dough too soft to handle.

THE LATTICE

On a floured surface, cut the second round of dough into eight wide strips. Lay four strips across the pie, evenly spaced. Peel back two "odd" strips and lay down the first of the perpendicular strips so it's under the "odd" strips and over the "even" strips. Repeat the process, peeling back the "even" strips this time for the second perpendicular strip to go under, and keep going in the same way with the last two perpendicular strips, continuing the alternation. Pinch the edges to seal them.

COOKING AND SERVING

Brush the pastry with the mixture of egg yolk and water, and sprinkle with the sugar. Place in the oven and bake for about 45 minutes. Allow the pie to cool for at least 4 hours before cutting.

HONEY PIE

A tribute to the perfect honey and butter pie from
Four & Twenty Blackbirds in Gowanus, Brooklyn.

MAKES ONE 10½ INCH PIE

Preparation time: 40 minutes, plus cooling
Resting time: 1 hour
Cooking time: about 1 hour

PASTRY

½ cup cold sweet/unsalted butter, diced
1½ cups all-purpose flour
¼ cup confectioners' sugar
½ teaspoon fine salt
4 tablespoons cold water
1 teaspoon cider vinegar
1 egg, beaten

FILLING

2¼ tablespoons fine cornmeal
4½ teaspoons cider vinegar
1 teaspoon natural vanilla extract
6 eggs
½ cup half and half, or whipping cream
1 pinch salt
⅓ cup sweet/unsalted butter
1½ cups light brown sugar (or 1¼ cups
    superfine sugar + 3 teaspoons molasses)
⅓ cup sugar syrup (page 176)
3½ oz light honey
4½ teaspoons fine sea salt

THE PASTRY

Using a food processor, cut the butter into the flour, confectioners' sugar, and salt, then incorporate the water and vinegar by hand just until you have a smooth dough. Roll into a ball, wrap it in plastic wrap and refrigerate for 1 hour.

SHAPING AND BLIND BAKING

Preheat the oven to 350°F. If the pastry dough is too hard when it comes out of the refrigerator, let it soften. Butter and flour a 10½ inch pie dish. On a floured surface, roll out the dough into a round large enough to hang over the edge of the dish by about 1¼ inches.
Place the round of dough in the dish, then roll the overhang onto itself and pinch with your fingers to shape the edge. Prick the pastry base with a fork, cover with parchment paper and dried beans, and bake for 15 minutes. Remove the paper and beans and brush the base with the beaten egg. Return to the oven for 2 minutes until dry and light golden, lowering the temperature to 325°F.

THE FILLING

Combine the cornmeal, vinegar, vanilla, eggs, cream, and salt.
In a pan, bring the butter, sugar, sugar syrup, and honey to a boil. Lower the heat and stir in the egg mixture, mixing with a spatula for about 5 minutes until you have a smooth cream. Do not boil.

ASSEMBLY AND COOKING

Preheat the oven to 350°F. Pour the filling into the pre-cooked pie shell. Bake for about 40 minutes until the filling is set, but still a little wobbly. Allow to cool and sprinkle with the fine sea salt.

PUMPKIN PIE

This smooth, delicious interpretation of the Thanksgiving classic is a gift from my friend Sara Jane Crawford, who has lent her baking skills to such fine establishments as the Rose Bakery in Paris and Marlow & Sons in South Williamsburg, Brooklyn.

MAKES ONE 10½ INCH PIE

Preparation time: 30 minutes, plus cooling
Resting time: 1 hour
Cooking time: about 1 hour 40 minutes

PASTRY

½ cup cold sweet/unsalted butter, diced
1⅓ cups all-purpose flour
½ teaspoon fine salt
5 tablespoons cold water
1 teaspoon lemon juice
1 egg, beaten

FILLING

3 eggs
1 egg yolk
⅔ cup light brown sugar (or ½ cup
    superfine sugar + 1 teaspoon molasses)
½ cup maple syrup
1½ cups half and half, or whipping cream
15 oz pumpkin purée*
1 teaspoon ground cinnamon
1 teaspoon ground ginger
½ teaspoon ground nutmeg

*You can use store-bought canned pumpkin purée, or make your own purée according to Sara's instructions.

THE PASTRY

Using a food processor, cut the butter into the flour and salt until the mixture is crumbly, then incorporate the water and lemon juice by hand, just until you have a smooth dough. Roll into a ball, wrap it in plastic wrap, and refrigerate for 1 hour.

SHAPING AND BLIND BAKING

Preheat the oven to 325°F. If the pastry dough is too hard when it comes out of the refrigerator, let it soften. Butter and flour a 10½ inch pie dish. On a floured surface, roll out the dough into a round large enough to hang over the edge of the dish by about 1¼ inches.
Place the round of dough in the dish, then roll the overhang onto itself and pinch with your fingers to shape the edge. Cover the pastry with parchment paper and dried beans, and bake for about 40 minutes until the edges are golden and the pastry is quite dry. Remove the paper and beans and brush the base with the beaten egg. Return to the oven for 2 minutes until dry and light golden.

THE FILLING

Preheat the oven to 350°F. Whisk together the eggs, egg yolk, and sugar. Incorporate the rest of the filling ingredients one by one and mix until combined. Pour the filling into the pastry shell and bake for about 40 minutes until the filling has set. Allow to cool before serving.

FOR HOMEMADE PUMPKIN PURÉE

Preheat the oven to 425°F. Peel a butternut squash (about 1 lb before cooking), remove the seeds, and cut into pieces. Place on a baking sheet lined with parchment paper, add enough water to cover the paper, and bake for about 1 hour, until the pumpkin flesh is very soft. Let the pieces of squash cool, then process them until you have a very smooth purée. If it is too watery, let it drain overnight in the refrigerator in a colander lined with a clean cotton dish towel.

CHINESE EGG CUSTARD TARTS

Warm custard tarts straight out of the steam oven are a staple of Chinatown coffee shops.
For the authentic shiny egg custard, you need to bake it slowly at a low temperature.

MAKES ABOUT 30 SMALL TARTS

Preparation time: 30 minutes
Resting time: 2–3 hours
Cooking time: 40 minutes

INNER "FAT" PASTRY

¾ cup sweet/unsalted butter,
    softened
6 oz coconut oil, soft or melted
1⅔ cups all-purpose flour

OUTER EGG PASTRY

1⅔ cups all-purpose flour
1 egg
⅓ cup iced water

FOR THE CUSTARD

⅔ cup sugar
1½ cups water
3 teaspoons cornstarch
6 tablespoons evaporated milk
4 eggs
4 egg yolks

THE PASTRIES

Combine all of the inner "fat" pastry ingredients together into a dough and refrigerate for 30 minutes.
Do the same for the outer egg pastry and refrigerate for 30 minutes as well.

SHAPING AND FOLDING

On a floured surface, roll out the first dough into a 8 inch square, then roll out the egg dough into a 12 inch square.
Place the smaller pastry square in the middle of the egg pastry square, so that the edges of the inside square are at a 45° angle to the edges of the outer square. Fold in the corners of the outer square over the inner square. Pinch the seams of the outer dough closed. Rest in the refrigerator for 30 minutes, then roll out the combined dough into a long rectangle, ¼ inch thick, making sure that the top and bottom edges of the rectangle are parallel to the rolling pin. Fold in each end like an envelope and return the dough to the refrigerator for another 30 minutes. Repeat the process two to four times, resting the pastry each time for 30 minutes.
Grease and flour 30 mini tart pans approximately 2½ inches along the base and 3½ inches in diameter (disposable foil pans or similar are ideal). To finish, roll out the pastry to a thickness of ¼ inch, and use a cutter to cut out circles that are large enough to line the pans. Place the circles of pastry into the pans and refrigerate.

THE CUSTARD

Preheat the oven to 350°F. In a saucepan, dissolve the sugar in the water over low heat and let it cool for 5 minutes. Blend the cornstarch with 1 tablespoon of the evaporated milk, then mix in the rest of the evaporated milk, the eggs, and the yolks. Whisk this mixture into the sugar water until combined.

COOKING

Place the pans lined with pastry on a baking sheet, fill them with the custard and bake, lowering the oven temperature to 300°F. Cook for 35 minutes until the filling is set but still a little wobbly.

Pastries + Food

Savory pies 6⁰⁰/7⁵⁰

Scones 3⁰⁰

Savory brioche 4⁰⁰

Savory bread 2⁵⁰

blackbird's bread 2⁵⁰

muffins 3⁰⁰

Cinnamon brioche 3⁰⁰

blackbird's granola
w/milk 4⁰⁰ w/yogurt 4⁵⁰

egg in a nest 4⁵⁰

CARROT CAKE

A cold slice of moist, spiced, carrot cake, with a thick topping of cream cheese frosting. What could be better?

MAKES ONE 8½ INCH CAKE

Preparation time: 30 minutes, plus cooling
Cooking time: 40 minutes

WET INGREDIENTS

¾ cup light brown sugar
    (or ½ cup superfine sugar
    + 2 teaspoons molasses)
½ cup sunflower oil
4 eggs
1½ tablespoons orange juice
zest of 1 orange, finely shredded
1 teaspoon natural vanilla extract

DRY INGREDIENTS

1½ cups all-purpose flour
2 teaspoons baking powder
3 pinches salt
2 teaspoons ground cinnamon
4 pinches ground nutmeg
4 pinches ground cardamom
4 pinches freshly ground black pepper

CARROTS, FRUIT, AND NUTS

1½ cups shredded carrot
2 tablespoons golden raisins
2 tablespoons chopped walnuts

FROSTING

½ cup sweet/unsalted butter, softened
5½ oz plain cream cheese, softened
    (such as Philadelphia®)
½ cup confectioners' sugar
1 cup shredded coconut (optional)

THE BATTER

Preheat the oven to 350°F. Beat the wet ingredients together vigorously. Combine the dry ingredients and add them to the wet mixture without overworking the batter. Finally, incorporate the carrots, fruit, and nuts. Butter and flour an 8½ inch cake pan. Pour in the batter and smooth the top.

COOKING

Bake for about 40 minutes until a skewer inserted into the middle of the cake comes out clean. Allow to cool.

THE FROSTING

Process the butter, cream cheese, and sugar in an electric mixer or beat with a wooden spoon until smooth and combined. Spread the frosting on the cake using a knife or spatula. Scatter over the shredded coconut, if using.

APPLE STRUDEL & CHERRY–RICOTTA STRUDEL

The flaky, buttery layers are the key to this traditional dessert from Central Europe.

MAKES 1 STRUDEL

Preparation time: 45 minutes, plus cooling
Cooking time: about 35 minutes

APPLE STRUDEL

3 tablespoons sweet/unsalted butter
5 Granny Smith apples, peeled, cored, and
    diced (about 13 oz prepared apple)
⅓ cup superfine sugar
2 teaspoons finely shredded lemon zest
½ cup flaked almonds
1 teaspoon natural vanilla extract
1½ teaspoons cornstarch
1½ tablespoons lemon juice

CHERRY–RICOTTA STRUDEL

14 oz ricotta cheese
¼ cup superfine sugar
5 teaspoons cornstarch
2 egg whites
6 oz frozen sour cherries, thawed, or
    6 oz fresh cherries, pitted and halved
½ cup all-purpose flour

PASTRY FOR ONE STRUDEL

½ cup dry breadcrumbs
½ cup superfine sugar
1½ teaspoons ground cinnamon for the
    apple strudel, or 1 vanilla bean, split
    lengthwise and seeds scraped, for the
    cherry strudel
4 sheets filo pastry
½ cup sweet/unsalted butter, melted

THE APPLE STRUDEL FILLING

Heat the butter in a frying pan over medium–high heat. At the first sizzle, add the apple and sugar. Sauté for 3 minutes. Add the lemon zest, almonds, and vanilla, and continue cooking until the apples are lightly browned on all sides.

Blend the cornstarch in with the lemon juice, and then add the entire mixture to the apples. Cook for another 5 minutes, stirring. Allow to cool.

THE CHERRY–RICOTTA STRUDEL FILLING

In a mixing bowl, whisk together the ricotta, sugar, cornstarch, and egg whites. When the mixture is smooth, warm it over low heat in a saucepan for 5 minutes to thicken it a little. Allow to cool.

Toss the cherries in the flour, then shake them a little to remove any excess flour.

ASSEMBLY

Preheat the oven to 400°F. Combine the breadcrumbs, sugar, and cinnamon if making the apple strudel, or the breadcrumbs, sugar, and vanilla bean seeds if making the cherry strudel.

Lay the first sheet of filo on a baking sheet lined with parchment paper. Brush it with melted butter and sprinkle with the breadcrumb mixture. Place another sheet on top and repeat the process with the remaining sheets of filo pastry and breadcrumb mixture, reserving a little mixture for the top. For the apple strudel, spread the apple filling into a sausage shape along one long side of the sheets of filo and roll up to enclose the filling.

For the cherry–ricotta strudel, spread the ricotta filling over the entire surface of the filo sheets, leaving a 1¼ inch border around the edges. Place two rows of the lightly floured cherries on the ricotta filling, one about one-third along the width of the filo sheets, the second two-thirds along. Roll the filo sheets up widthwise to form a sausage.

COOKING

Brush the surface of the strudel with the remaining melted butter and sprinkle with the remaining breadcrumb mixture. Bake for about 22 minutes. Allow to cool and serve in slices.

NEW YORK CHEESECAKE

The genuine article, like the one you can eat at Junior's in Brooklyn.

MAKES ONE 11¼ INCH CHEESECAKE

Preparation time: 25 minutes
Cooking time: 1 hour 15 minutes
Resting time in the oven: 2 hours
Refrigeration time: 4 hours

CRUST

6½ oz Graham Crackers®, crushed
1 tablespoon superfine sugar
⅓ cup sweet/unsalted butter, melted

CHEESE FILLING

2 lb plain cream cheese, softened
    (preferably Philadelphia®)
1¼ cups superfine sugar
½ teaspoon salt
½ cup all-purpose flour
1 lemon, juice, and finely
    shredded zest
1 lb 5 oz sour cream
8 eggs
1 teaspoon natural vanilla extract

THE CRUST

Grease the base and side of an 11¼ inch springform cake pan. Preheat the oven to 350°F. Combine the crushed Graham Crackers, sugar, and melted butter, then spread this mixture over the base, pressing it down well with the bottom of a glass. Place in the oven and bake for 15 minutes. Take the crust out of the oven and increase the temperature to 450°F.

THE CHEESE FILLING

Using an electric mixer or food processor, combine the filling ingredients, in the order they are listed, until smooth. Pour over the crust.

COOKING

Bake for 10 minutes. Without opening the oven, lower the temperature to 200°F and cook for another 50 minutes. The filling should still be a little wobbly in the center. Turn the oven off and let the cheesecake rest inside for 2 hours, then let it cool outside of the oven and refrigerate for at least 4 hours before serving.

ITALIAN-STYLE CHEESECAKE

This is the other great New York cheesecake. Unlike its better-known rival, which is made with cream cheese, the Italian version is made with ricotta cheese, resulting in a lighter, slightly wet, consistency.

MAKES TWO 4½ INCH CHEESECAKES

Preparation time: 25 minutes, plus cooling
Cooking time: 15 minutes

CRUST

¾ cup all-purpose flour
½ teaspoon salt
1¾ oz ricotta cheese
3 tablespoons sweet/unsalted butter, softened
¾ cup confectioners' sugar

CHEESE FILLING

1 lb ricotta cheese
½ cup superfine sugar
3 tablespoons all-purpose flour
2 eggs
1 pinch salt
¼ cup lemon juice or pastis (anise-flavored liqueur)
½ teaspoon natural vanilla extract

DECORATION

⅔ cup strawberries
confectioners' sugar for dusting

THE CRUST

Preheat the oven to 450°F. Mix the ingredients for the crust using a food processor, or by hand until combined. Butter and flour the base and one-third of the way up the sides of two 4½ inch springform cake pans, then spread the mixture over the base.

THE CHEESE FILLING

Whisk together the cheese filling ingredients until smooth, then pour equal amounts over the two crusts.

COOKING

Bake the cheesecakes for about 15 minutes. When they come out of the oven, the filling should still be wobbly in the center. Allow to cool.

THE DECORATION

Arrange slices of strawberry on top of each cheesecake

CHOCOLATE CUPCAKES

The following are my three favorite cupcake recipes.
Feel free to mix and match the batter and frosting recipes in different ways.

MAKES ABOUT 18 CUPCAKES

Preparation time: 25 minutes, plus cooling
Cooking time: 20 minutes

INGREDIENTS FOR MELTING

7 oz dark/semiweet chocolate, cut
   into pieces
1 cup sweet/unsalted butter
4½ teaspoons cocoa powder

INGREDIENTS FOR WHISKING

6 eggs, separated
1 cup superfine sugar

DRY INGREDIENTS

1 cup + 1 tablespoon all-purpose flour
1 pinch salt

COFFEE FROSTING

½ cup sweet/unsalted butter, softened
1¾ cups confectioners' sugar
1 oz light brown sugar
3 tablespoons cold espresso coffee
1 teaspoon coffee extract

THE CHOCOLATE CUPCAKE

Preheat the oven to 315°F.
In a saucepan, melt the pieces of chocolate with the butter
and cocoa powder, stirring regularly. Remove from heat.
Whisk together the egg yolks and sugar until thick and pale.
Beat the egg whites until stiff peaks form.
Combine the dry ingredients in a bowl. Gradually add the
combined dry ingredients to the egg yolk and sugar mixture.
Mix well, then pour in the melted chocolate–butter mixture while
stirring. Carefully fold in the beaten egg whites using a spatula.
Fill muffin pans with paper liners and divide the batter between
them. Cook in the oven for about 20 minutes. Allow to cool. Turn
out the cupcakes and spread frosting on each one using a spatula.

THE COFFEE FROSTING

Beat the butter and sugars together in a food processor or with
a spatula until smooth. Add the coffee and the coffee extract and
mix again vigorously in the processor or with the spatula for at least
5 minutes until the mixture becomes creamy. It is then ready to use.

VANILLA CUPCAKES

MAKES ABOUT 20 CUPCAKES

Preparation time: 20 minutes, plus cooling
Cooking time: 25 minutes

DRY INGREDIENTS

1⅔ cups all-purpose flour
2¼ teaspoons baking powder
1 pinch salt

INGREDIENTS FOR WHISKING

6 eggs
1½ teaspoons natural vanilla extract
1 teaspoon finely shredded orange zest
1 cup sweet/unsalted butter,
    at room temperature
1 cup superfine sugar

VANILLA FROSTING

½ cup sweet/unsalted butter, softened
2 cups confectioners' sugar
1 tablespoon milk
½ vanilla bean, split lengthwise and
    seeds scraped

THE VANILLA CUPCAKE

Preheat the oven to 315°F.
Combine the dry ingredients. Using an electric mixer,
beat the eggs, vanilla, and zest on a high speed until light and fluffy.
Whisk the softened butter and sugar together vigorously, then
alternately add the combined dry ingredients and the egg mixture.
Carefully combine.
Fill silicon molds or two muffin pans with paper liners and divide
the batter between them.
Cook in the oven for about 25 minutes. Allow to cool. Turn out
the cupcakes and spread frosting on each one using a spatula.

THE VANILLA FROSTING

Beat the butter and sugar together in a food processor or with a spatula
until smooth. Add the milk and the vanilla bean seeds and mix again
vigorously in the processor or with the spatula for at least 5 minutes.
The mixture will become creamy and is then ready to use.

MATCHA CUPCAKES

MAKES ABOUT 20 CUPCAKES

Preparation time: 20 minutes, plus cooling
Cooking time: 25 minutes

DRY INGREDIENTS

1⅔ cups all-purpose flour
4½ teaspoons matcha green tea powder
2¼ teaspoons baking powder
1 pinch salt

INGREDIENTS FOR WHISKING

6 eggs
1 cup sweet/unsalted butter,
   at room temperature
1 cup superfine sugar

RASPBERRY FROSTING

4½ oz raspberry jam
½ cup sweet/unsalted butter, softened
1¾ cups confectioners' sugar

THE MATCHA CUPCAKE

Preheat the oven to 315°F.
Combine the dry ingredients. Using an electric mixer, beat
the eggs on a high speed until light and fluffy. Whisk the softened butter
and sugar together vigorously, then alternately add the combined dry
ingredients and the eggs. Carefully combine.
Fill silicon molds, or two muffin pans, with paper liners and divide the
batter between them.
Cook in the oven for about 25 minutes. Allow to cool. Turn out
the cupcakes and spread frosting on each one using a spatula.

THE RASPBERRY FROSTING

Heat the raspberry jam in a small saucepan, strain to remove the seeds,
then cool.
Beat the butter and sugar together in a food processor or with a spatula
until smooth. Add the strained raspberry jam and mix again vigorously
for at least 5 minutes. The mixture will become creamy and is then
ready to use.

DOODLES

For a different cupcake experience, use the batter and frosting recipes from the previous pages to make inside-out cupcakes.

THE BATTER

When you make cupcakes, you try to achieve a top that's nice and flat. When you make doodles, which aren't frosted, you want them to be more rounded. To do that, I cook them in a hotter oven but for a shorter time.

So it's just the cooking that's different.

CHOCOLATE DOODLES

325°F for 23 minutes.

VANILLA DOODLES

325°F for 24 minutes.

MATCHA DOODLES

325°F for 24 minutes.

THE FROSTING

Once the doodles have cooled, make holes in the middle of the top using a chopstick or skewer. Fill an icing bag, fitted with a plain nozzle, with frosting and fill the inside of the doodles.

FLOURLESS CHOCOLATE CAKE

The inspiration for this cake is the mousse-like chocolate cake at Diner, in Williamsburg, Brooklyn. It's an intense, light, pure, chocolate experience.

MAKES ONE 9½ INCH CAKE

Preparation time: 20 minutes, plus cooling
Cooking time: about 1 hour

INGREDIENTS

½ cup sweet/unsalted butter + extra for greasing the pan
10½ oz dark/semisweet chocolate
1½ tablespoons cocoa powder
6 eggs, separated
½ cup superfine sugar + extra for dusting the pan
1 pinch salt
5½ oz sour cream
½ teaspoon natural vanilla extract

THE PAN

Preheat the oven to 300°F. Wrap foil around the seams of a 9½ inch springform cake pan so you can bake the cake in a bain-marie (water bath). Cover the inside of the pan with a thick layer of softened butter. Sprinkle some sugar for dusting on the butter and tilt the pan to distribute the sugar evenly, shaking out the excess.

THE MIXTURE

Melt the butter, chocolate, and cocoa powder together over low heat, in a double boiler or in the microwave. Beat the egg whites with half the sugar and the salt until stiff peaks form. Beat the yolks with the remaining sugar, sour cream, and vanilla until smooth.
Combine the egg yolk mixture with the melted chocolate mixture, then fold in the egg white mixture until the mixture is incorporated.

COOKING AND SERVING

Pour the batter into the pan and place the pan inside a larger baking dish. Pour boiling water into the larger dish to three-quarters of the height of the cake pan. Bake for 55 minutes or until a skewer inserted into the middle of the cake comes out clean. Remove the bain-marie from the oven, leaving the cake in it for 3 more minutes. Remove the cake from the bain-marie and allow to cool.
Serve chilled with whipped cream (page 263).

GOOD POPS

Popsicles (or Bobsicles, in this case)
are the perfect summer treat. Here are
a few easy and delicious fruit-based
recipes from the barman/manager at
Bob's Juice Bar: Jean-Pierre Ahtuam.

FOR 6 LARGE POPSICLES
Preparation time: 5 minutes
Freezing time: at least 8 hours

In each case, you simply blend everything together
in a blender or food processor, as you would for
a smoothie. Fill molds with the mixture, insert popsicle
sticks or handles in the top, then seal, and freeze.
You can use store-bought molds with built-in handles,
or use disposable cups or recycled dessert containers
as molds, as I've done for the "bad pops," page 210.
Freeze the popsicles for at least 8 hours. Take the
popsicle out of the freezer to warm up for a few
minutes before trying to sink your teeth into it.

STRAWBERRY
3 tablespoons maple
    syrup or sugar syrup
1 cup water
13 oz strawberries

WATERMELON
¼ cup maple syrup or
    sugar syrup
1 lb 4 oz watermelon
6 mint leaves

MANGO LASSI
11¼ oz mango
11¼ oz yogurt
1 teaspoon honey
seeds of 2 cardamom
    pods

CANTELOUPE
1 lb 4 oz canteloupe
3½ oz banana

LEMONADE
2 cups lemon juice
1 cup maple syrup or
    sugar syrup

BLUEBERRY YOGURT
8 oz blueberries
11¼ oz yogurt
¼ cup maple syrup or
    sugar syrup

BLUEBERRY SMOOTHIE
5¾ oz blueberries
5¾ oz banana
1⅓ cups orange juice

note: *To make sugar syrup see page 176.*

BAD POPS

Here are two non-fruit popsicles that never fail to satisfy.

CHOCOLATE POPSICLES

MAKES 6

Preparation time: 10 minutes
Cooking time: 10 minutes
Freezing time: at least 8 hours

INGREDIENTS

1½ tablespoons cornstarch
⅔ cup milk
1¼ cups half and half
2 pinches salt
¼ cup cocoa powder
⅓ cup superfine sugar
1 oz dark/semisweet chocolate,
   chopped
1 teaspoon natural vanilla extract

THE CREAM

Make a slurry from the cornstarch and 2 tablespoons of milk.
Add the rest of the milk, mix and set aside.
In a saucepan over low heat, whisk together the cream, salt,
cocoa, and sugar. Reduce the heat when it starts to boil. Add
the milk–cornstarch mixture, continuing to whisk.
When the mixture starts to thicken, remove from the heat, and
mix in the chocolate pieces and vanilla. Stir until melted and smooth.

SETTING AND SERVING

Pour into popsicle molds, cool, then secure the popsicle sticks,
cover, and freeze for at least 8 hours.

note: *This popsicle is also known as a "fudgesicle."*

COFFEE POPSICLES

MAKES 6

Preparation time: 10 minutes
Freezing time: at least 8 hours

INGREDIENTS

1 cup sweetened condensed milk
1¾ cups strong cold coffee

Whisk together the condensed milk and coffee until smooth.
Pour into popsicle molds, secure the popsicle sticks, cover, and
freeze for at least 8 hours.

note: *For the popsicles you see in the photo, I used takeout espresso cups with*
matching lids that I poked the sticks through. You could do the same thing with
another homemade solution such as recycled yogurt containers with some foil, or
use store-bought popsicle molds with the sticks built in.

HOMEMADE GRAHAM CRACKERS®

This honey-flavored treat is a key ingredient in cheesecakes and s'mores. It is also delicious to munch all on its own.

MAKES ABOUT 32 CRACKERS

Preparation time: 20 minutes, plus cooling
Refrigeration time: at least 1 hour
Cooking time: about 15 minutes

WET INGREDIENTS

¼ cup sweet/unsalted butter, softened
⅔ cup light brown sugar (or ½ cup
    superfine sugar + 2 teaspoons molasses)
1 egg
1½ tablespoons honey
1½ tablespoons milk

DRY INGREDIENTS

1 teaspoon baking powder
½ teaspoon salt
1⅔ cups whole-wheat flour

THE PASTRY

Beat the butter and sugar in an electric mixer or by hand until light and creamy. Whisk together the egg, honey, and milk. Combine all the dry ingredients.
Add the egg mixture to the butter mixture alternately with the dry ingredients until you have a smooth dough. Form into a ball, cover loosely in plastic wrap, and refrigerate for at least 1 hour.

SHAPING THE PASTRY

Preheat the oven to 350°F. Divide the dough into two balls. Roll out one ball thinly to about ¹⁄₁₆ inch thick on a baking sheet lined with parchment paper. Using a pastry cutter or a knife, score the rolled-out dough into 16 rectangles of the same size. Using the tip of a knife, make lines of small holes on the crackers.

COOKING

Bake for about 15 minutes until the crackers are golden brown. As soon as they come out of the oven, separate the crackers using a dough cutter following the marks made before cooking. Allow to cool on the baking sheet and set the crackers aside. Repeat the process with the second ball of dough.

note: *Reserve any off-cuts to crush and use as a base for cheesecakes (page 196) or tarts.*

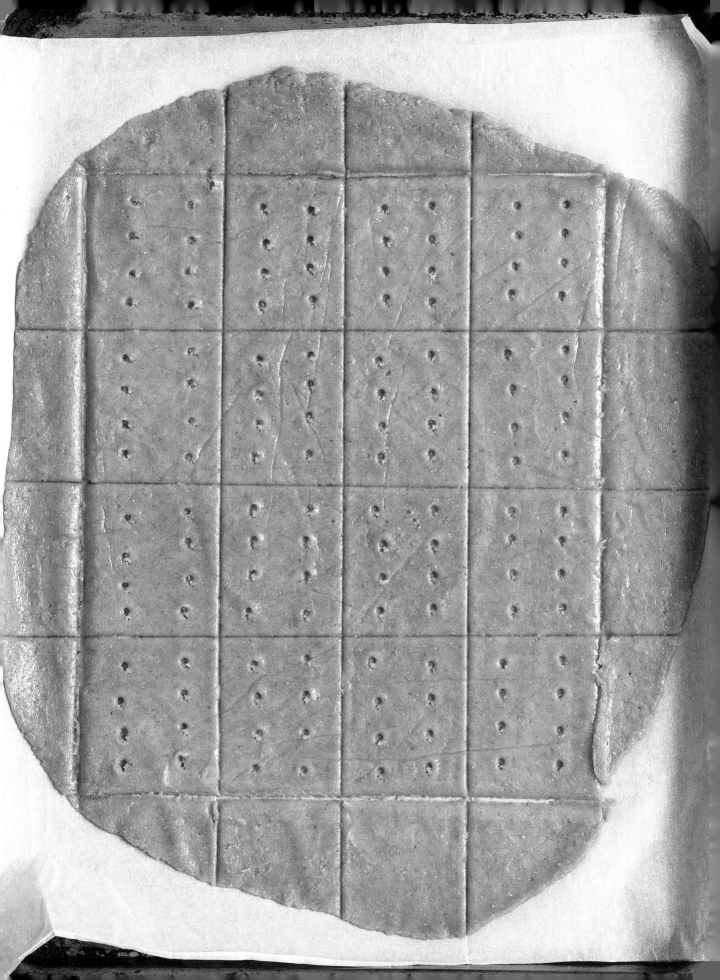

S'MORES

When I was a kid, we made s'mores at summer camp around the fire, toasting marshmallows on sticks, and then sandwiching them with chocolate between two Graham Crackers®.

MAKES 1 S'MORE

Preparation time: 5 minutes
Cooking time: 5 minutes

INGREDIENTS

2 homemade extra-large Graham Crackers®
    (page 212), or other sweet whole wheat crackers
4 squares of dark/semisweet chocolate (enough
    to cover a cracker)
Marshmallows (page 232)

Preheat the oven broiler. Place crackers on a baking sheet lined with parchment paper, top them with squares of chocolate, and a marshmallow the same size as the cracker. Place the cracker under the broiler and watch it carefully so that it doesn't burn. After about a minute, the marshmallow will start to color and smell like caramel, as the chocolate will start to melt. Remove from the broiler, top with the second cracker, and serve immediately.

extra large Graham Crackers®: Graham Crackers® are the crackers used for s'mores. To make extra-large s'mores, just make your homemade Graham Crackers® thicker and wider. Roll out the dough until about ¼ inch thick and cut into rectangles about 4 x 3¼ inches. Cook them for 18–20 minutes until they're golden brown. Separate crackers with a pastry cutter as soon as they come out of the oven, and let them cool on a rack. You need two crackers to make a s'more.

WHOOPIE PIES

*"Makin' whoopee" means to make love, and eating these light
and airy Amish cakes is effectively an ecstatic experience.*

MAKES 14 WHOOPIE PIES

Preparation time: 30 minutes, plus cooling
Cooking time: 8 minutes

COOKIES

1⅓ cups all-purpose flour

3 teaspoons baking powder

1¼ oz cocoa powder

3 oz coconut oil, at room temperature,
    or sweet/unsalted butter, softened

⅔ cup light brown sugar (or ½ cup
    superfine sugar + 2 teaspoons molasses)

2 egg yolks

1 pinch salt

¼ cup water

FILLING

2 egg whites

2 pinches salt

¼ cup cold sugar syrup (page 176)

¾ cup confectioners' sugar

1 teaspoon natural vanilla extract

THE COOKIE BATTER

Preheat the oven to 400°F. Combine the flour, baking powder, and
cocoa. In a food processor or by hand, beat the coconut oil and sugar
vigorously until light and creamy. Incorporate the egg yolks, then
the flour mixture, the salt, and finally the water, continuing to beat
until you have a smooth batter.

COOKING

Using a spoon or an icing bag fitted with a plain nozzle, pipe tablespoons
of mixture on two baking sheets lined with parchment paper, leaving
1¼ inches between each. Bake for about 8 minutes until the cookies are
well risen and quite firm. Allow to cool.

THE FILLING

Using an electric beater, whisk the egg whites with the salt and, when
they begin to froth up, gradually incorporate the sugar syrup. When the
mixture has doubled in volume, gradually add the confectioners' sugar
and the vanilla, continuing to whisk until the consistency of the mixture
is smooth and mousse-like.

ASSEMBLY

Using a spoon or an icing bag, spread the filling on half of the cookies,
then top with the remaining cookies.

*note: If you want to make elongated whoopie pies, like Devil Dogs®
use the icing bag to form small sausages.*

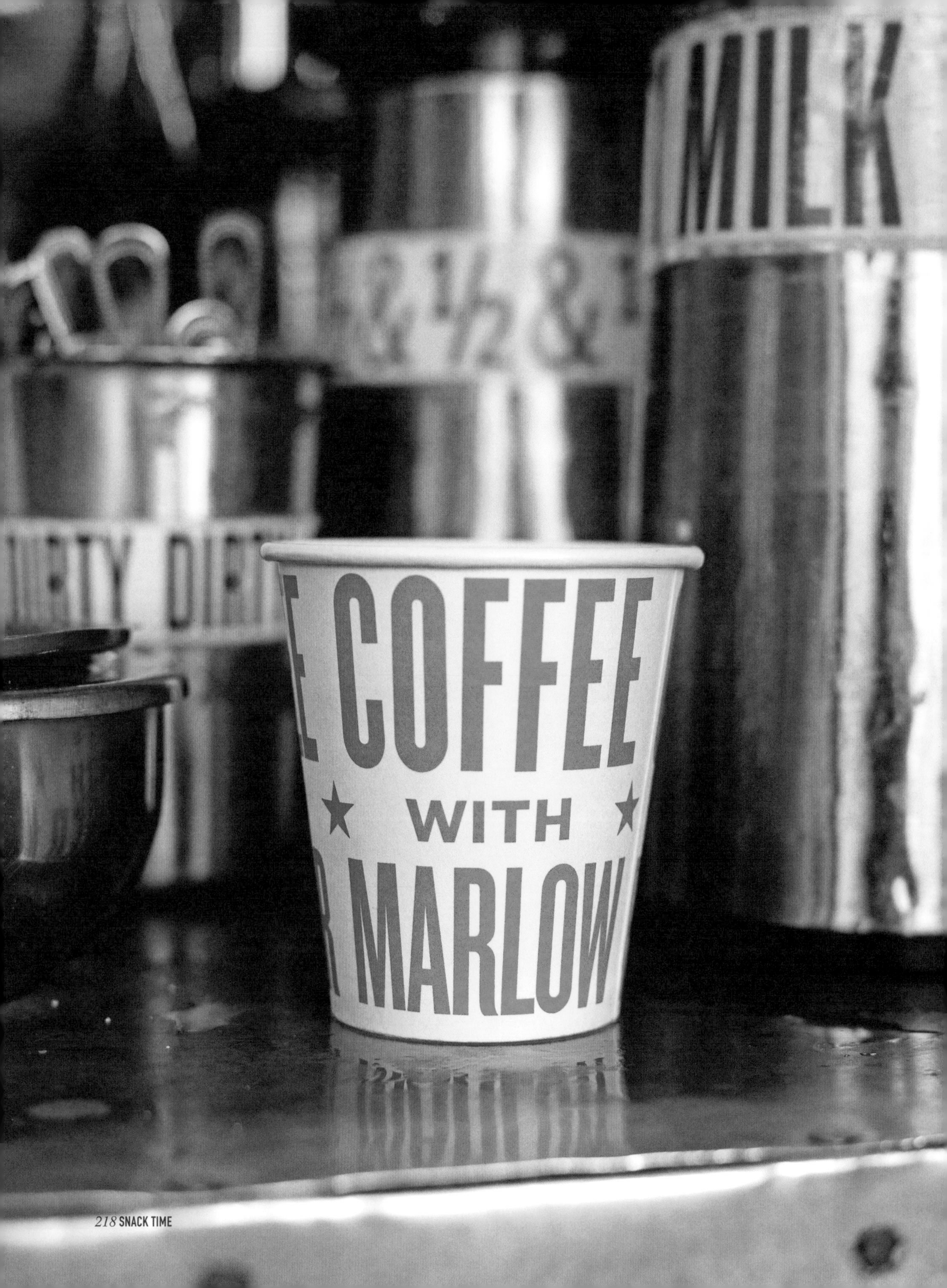
MILK
COFFEE
WITH
MARLOW

BLONDIES

MAKES 16 SQUARES

Preparation time: 20 minutes, plus cooling
Cooking time: 32 minutes

INGREDIENTS FOR WHISKING

⅔ cup sweet/unsalted butter
⅓ cup sunflower oil
1½ cups light brown sugar
2 eggs
1 teaspoon natural vanilla extract

DRY INGREDIENTS

2 cups all-purpose flour
2 teaspoons baking powder
½ teaspoon salt
2½ oz white chocolate, chopped,
   (or white chocolate chips)
3½ oz pecans, chopped

THE BATTER

Preheat the oven to 350°F. In a saucepan, melt the
butter over low heat and whisk vigorously for a few
minutes with the oil, sugar, eggs, and vanilla. Remove
from the heat. Combine the dry ingredients, then stir
in the butter mixture.

COOKING

Butter and flour a 9½ inch square cake pan. Pour the
batter into the pan. With a wet hand, flatten and
smooth the surface. Bake for about 30 minutes. The
cake should be fairly firm to the touch. Allow to cool,
then cut into 16 squares.

BROWNIES

A brownie should be dense, chewy, and have a thin, shiny crust on top. You can add nuts if you want. Personally, I prefer to double the amount of chocolate.

MAKES 16 SQUARES

Preparation time: 25 minutes, plus cooling
Cooking time: 40 minutes

INGREDIENTS FOR MELTING

½ cup sweet/unsalted butter
11½ oz dark/semisweet chocolate
1 oz cocoa powder

INGREDIENTS FOR WHISKING

¼ cup sunflower oil
1⅓ cups light brown sugar (or 1¼ cups
    superfine sugar + 3 teaspoons molasses)
½ teaspoon natural vanilla extract
3 eggs
3 egg yolks

DRY INGREDIENTS

1 cup all-purpose flour
½ teaspoon salt
⅔ cup chopped dark/semisweet chocolate

THE BATTER

Preheat the oven to 350°F. In a saucepan, melt the butter, chocolate, and cocoa powder over low heat. In a bowl, whisk the oil, sugar, vanilla, eggs, and egg yolks vigorously for a few minutes. Combine the dry ingredients and add them to the whisked mixture, then stir in the melted mixture.

COOKING

Grease and flour a 9 inch square baking pan. Spread the batter in the pan. With a wet hand, flatten and smooth the surface. Bake for about 35 minutes. The top of the cake will become shiny and start to crack, and it should be fairly solid to the touch. Allow to cool and cut into 16 squares.

BROOKLYN CAFÉS

Four & Twenty Blackbirds and Bakeri: These two bakery–cafés are emblems of the "homemade" ethos and sexy "low-tech" ambience that has made Brooklyn the hippest neighborhood in New York.

OPEN DAI
8 to 7

CHOCOLATE CHIP COOKIES

I use the same basic recipe to make two versions of this classic cookie:
An extra-large one, overloaded with huge and irregular chunks
of chocolate, and another, mini-sized one, with chocolate chips.

MAKES 18 BIG COOKIES OR 45 MINI COOKIES

Preparation time: 25 minutes, plus cooling
Refrigeration time: 2 hours
Cooking time: 10 minutes

WET INGREDIENTS

1 cup sweet/unsalted butter, softened
⅔ cup superfine sugar
½ cup light brown sugar (or ⅓ cup
　superfine sugar + 1 teaspoon molasses)
1 teaspoon natural vanilla extract
2 pinches salt
2 eggs

DRY INGREDIENTS

2⅔ cups all-purpose flour
1 teaspoon baking powder
7 oz chocolate, coarsely chopped into
　chunks (or 1⅔ cups chocolate chips
　for the mini ones)
⅓ cup chopped macadamia nuts
　or walnuts (or ⅓ cup extra pieces
　of chocolate)
1 teaspoon fine sea salt (optional)

THE DOUGH

Beat the butter and sugars in a food processor or by hand until light and creamy. Add the other wet ingredients, beating constantly until smooth.

Combine the dry ingredients—if making mini cookies, substitute the coarsely chopped chocolate with chocolate chips and omit the nuts. Combine the two mixtures until a dough forms. Shape into a ball, cover loosely in plastic wrap, and refrigerate for 1 hour.

SHAPING INTO A SAUSAGE (FOR THE BIG ONES)

Take the dough out of the refrigerator, remove the plastic wrap, and place the dough on a sheet of parchment paper. With the help of the parchment paper, shape the dough into a smooth sausage shape about 4 inches in diameter. Wrap the dough in the sheet of parchment paper and refrigerate for at least 1 hour.

COOKING

Preheat the oven to 400°F. Remove the dough sausage from the refrigerator and unwrap from the parchment paper. Using a knife or a pastry cutter, cut it into round slices about ⅝ inch thick, if making big cookies.

Arrange them on a baking sheet lined with parchment paper. Bake for about 10 minutes, then allow to cool for at least 10 minutes at room temperature before serving.

If making mini cookies, roll heaped teaspoons of dough into balls and bake for 5–6 minutes. The cookies should still be slightly soft when they come out of the oven. Allow them to cool for at least 10 minutes at room temperature before serving.

note: *I discovered the extra touch that sea salt gives from eating a great David's-style chocolate chip cookie at the incredible Bakeri in Williamsburg. Since then, no chocolate chip cookie seems complete to me without this little pinch.*

BLACK & WHITE COOKIES

The ultimate New York cookie.

MAKES 9 LARGE COOKIES

Preparation time: 30 minutes, plus cooling
Cooking time: 15 minutes

DOUGH

⅓ cup sweet/unsalted butter, softened
½ cup superfine sugar
2 eggs
¼ cup buttermilk
½ teaspoon natural vanilla extract
½ teaspoon finely shredded lemon zest
1⅔ cups all-purpose flour
1 teaspoon baking powder
1 pinch salt

WHITE FROSTING

1½ cups confectioners' sugar
1½ tablespoons boiling water

BLACK FROSTING

2 teaspoons sweet/unsalted butter
3 tablespoons half and half,
    or whipping cream
2¼ oz dark/semisweet chocolate, chopped
⅓ cup confectioners' sugar
1 teaspoon boiling water

THE DOUGH

Preheat the oven to 350°F. Using a food processor or a wooden spoon, beat the butter and sugar vigorously until light and creamy. Incorporate the eggs, buttermilk, and vanilla, continuing to beat until smooth. Next add the lemon zest and dry ingredients, and mix until you have a smooth dough.

COOKING

Roll 2 tablespoons of dough into balls to make each of about 9 cookies and place on a baking sheet lined with parchment paper, leaving 1¼ inches between each cookie. Bake for about 12 minutes until the cookies are lightly browned. Allow them to cool on a wire rack, then return them to the baking sheet.

THE FROSTING

Combine the white frosting ingredients until smooth. Using a brush or spoon, spread this frosting on one half of the flat side of each cookie. For the black frosting, place the butter and cream in a saucepan and bring to a boil over medium heat. Remove from the heat, add the chopped chocolate, and let it melt for 1 minute, then add the confectioners' sugar and boiling water. Spread the black frosting on the other half of the cookies. Lay the biscuits on a wire rack to let the frosting harden.

tip: If the frosting becomes too thick, add a little boiling water to make it easier to spread.

HOMEMADE OREOS®

Here is my recipe for Oreos®, recreating the traditional sandwich cookie.

MAKES ABOUT 16 HOMEMADE OREOS®

Preparation time: 25 minutes, plus cooling
Refrigeration time: 2 hours
Cooking time: 15 minutes

WET INGREDIENTS

⅔ cup sweet/unsalted butter, softened
1⅔ cups light brown sugar
   (or 1½ cups superfine sugar
   + 1 tablespoon molasses)
1 egg, beaten
1 teaspoon natural vanilla extract

DRY INGREDIENTS

1 cup + 1 tablespoon all-purpose flour
¾ cup cocoa powder
2 teaspoons baking powder
2 pinches salt

CREAM FILLING

5 teaspoons sweet/unsalted butter,
   softened
1 oz coconut oil, at room temperature
1 cup confectioners' sugar

THE DOUGH

Using an electric mixer, beat the butter and sugar vigorously until light and creamy. Combine all the dry ingredients. Add to the butter–sugar mixture, alternating with the beaten egg and vanilla until smooth.
Shape into a ball, cover loosely in plastic wrap, and refrigerate for at least 1 hour.

SHAPING THE DOUGH

Take the dough out of the refrigerator, remove the plastic wrap, and place the dough on a sheet of parchment paper. With the help of the parchment paper, shape the dough into a smooth sausage shape about 12 inches long. Wrap the dough in the sheet of parchment paper and refrigerate for at least 1 hour.

COOKING

Preheat the oven to 350°F. Remove the dough sausage from the refrigerator and unwrap it from the parchment paper. Using a large knife or a pastry cutter, cut slices about ½ inch thick. Arrange them on two baking sheets lined with parchment paper, leaving a ¾ inch space between each. Flatten them slightly with your hands to give them a round and smooth shape, then bake for 15 minutes. Allow to cool at room temperature.

THE CREAM FILLING

Combine all the ingredients with a whisk until smooth and creamy.

ASSEMBLY

Turn over half the batch of cookies, flat side facing up. Place about 2½ teaspoons of the cream filling in the middle of each and top with the other half. Press the two cookies together until the cream reaches the edge.

note: For a fluted edge, roll out the dough until ½ inch thick and cut out the cookies with a fluted cookie cutter.

ice cream version: You can also use the cookies to make ice cream sandwiches. Put 1 spoonful of ice cream on the flat side of one cookie and top with another cookie, then wrap the sandwich in a double layer of parchment paper and foil and store the wrapped ice cream sandwich in the freezer until ready to serve.

MARSHMALLOWS

Homemade marshmallows are a real treat. As with other homemade versions of typically mass-produced foods, making your own means you can be sure that the ingredients are of good quality and customize the recipe to your liking.

SERVES 2

Preparation time: 20 minutes
Cooking time: 20 minutes
Setting time: 5 hours

INGREDIENTS

⅔ cup confectioners' sugar
4½ teaspoons cornstarch
1¼ oz powdered gelatin
1 cup water
1 lb sugar
6 oz light corn syrup
2 egg whites
1 pinch salt
3 teaspoons natural vanilla extract
(or other flavoring such as rose
syrup, orange blossom water,
coffee extract, etc.)

THE PAN

Combine the confectioners' sugar and cornstarch. Oil a 10 inch square baking pan and sift about three-quarters of the sugar–cornstarch mixture over the oiled surface.

THE MIXTURE

Sprinkle the gelatin over half the water. Place the sugar, corn syrup, and the remaining water in a saucepan over medium heat, stirring until the sugar dissolves. Bring to a boil, then lower the heat to keep on a very gentle simmer for about 15 minutes without stirring. Periodically wipe down the side of the saucepan with a wet pastry brush to clean off any crystallized sugar. Using a food thermometer, monitor the temperature of the mixture—it should reach 250°F—then remove from the heat. Add the gelatin to the sugar mixture, mixing with a fork or whisk until it is completely dissolved.

Beat the egg whites in an electric mixer with the pinch of salt until stiff peaks form, and set aside. Beat the gelatin–sugar syrup with an electric beater until it has more than doubled in size. Incorporate the beaten egg whites, then the vanilla or other flavor, and continue to beat until combined.

SETTING AND SERVING

Pour the mixture into the pan, smooth the top, and dust with the rest of the sugar–cornstarch mixture. Let it sit for 5 hours at room temperature. Turn out the mixture and cut into small cubes. Store covered in the refrigerator.

HOT COCOA & MARSH-MALLOWS

Not to be confused with hot chocolate. The marshmallows on top are really key in this recipe.

SERVES 2
Preparation time: 5 minutes
Cooking time: 5 minutes

INGREDIENTS
1½ tablespoons good quality cocoa powder
¼ cup sweetened condensed milk
½ teaspoon natural vanilla extract
1 pinch salt
1¾ cups water
marshmallows (as many as you like)

THE HOT COCOA
Combine the cocoa powder with 1½ tablespoons of the sweetened condensed milk. Add the remaining condensed milk, vanilla, and salt, then pour everything into a saucepan and heat over medium heat. Gradually add the water, mixing with a spatula. Heat to just below boiling point and serve with marshmallows.

MUFFINS
See "banana bread" recipe page 30.

24/24
ANY TIME

EGG IN A HOLE

If you like toast dipped in egg yolk (and who doesn't?), this recipe, also known as Toad in the Hole, is for you.

MAKES 1 EGG IN A HOLE

Preparation time: 5 minutes
Cooking time: 2 minutes

INGREDIENTS

1 slice sandwich bread
1 egg
3 teaspoons butter

THE HOLE IN THE BREAD

Using a round cookie or biscuit cutter cut out and remove a circle from the middle of the slice of bread. Place the slice of bread and the circle in a dish. Break an egg, being careful not to break the yolk, and let most of the white out into the dish with the bread, leaving the rest of the white and the yolk in the shell.

Soak the slice of bread and the bread circle in the egg white, turning it over after about 1 minute.

COOKING

Melt the butter in a frying pan over medium heat and, when it starts to sizzle, add the slice of bread. Gently pour the yolk and the rest of the egg white into the hole.

After about 1 minute, slide a thin spatula under the bread and gently turn it over onto the other side. Brown for about 1 minute. The aim is to fill and seal the hole with egg without drying out the yolk. Season with salt and pepper.

PICKLES

In a world obsessed with speed, it's good to know that places like The Pickle Guys still exist. They make pickles, just like in the old days, taking their time, fermenting Kirby cucumbers, and other fruits and vegetables, for up to three months in refrigerated barrels.

FAST PICKLES

Here are a few of my favorite vinegar pickle recipes.
They are much quicker to make than fermented pickles.

FOR 4½ OZ PICKLES

Preparation time: 10 minutes
Cooking time: 5 minutes
Resting time: 24 hours

INGREDIENTS

4½ oz vegetables and/or fruit
2 teaspoons pickling spices
    (peppercorns, mustard
    seeds, allspice)
1 bay leaf

BRINE INGREDIENTS

½ cup water
1½ tablespoons vinegar
1 teaspoon of non-iodized coarse salt
2 teaspoons sugar (optional)

Clean and chop up, or slice, the vegetables and/or fruit, and place them in a heat-resistant container. Add the spices and bay leaf. Combine the water, vinegar, salt, and sugar in a saucepan over medium heat. Bring to a boil while stirring. Pour the hot brine into the container. Cover and allow to cool, then refrigerate for 24 hours before serving.

VARIATIONS

spiced pineapple: *Rice or cider vinegar, extra 1–2 teaspoons of sugar.*
Additional ingredient: 2 dried chilis.

red onion: *Red wine vinegar.*
Additional ingredients: 1 slice cooked red beet for color, 3 cloves.

radish: *Rice or cider vinegar.*

short cucumber: *Rice or cider vinegar.*
Additional ingredient: 1 garlic clove.

green mango: *Rice or cider vinegar.*
Additional ingredients: 3 cardamom pods, 2 dried chilis.

carrot: *Rice or cider vinegar.*
Additional ingredients: 3 cardamom pods, 3 cloves.

SLOW PICKLES

Here is a recipe for traditional saltwater pickles, like the ones made by
The Pickle Guys on the Lower East Side of Manhattan, and served in most
New York delis and diners. Feel free to adjust the mix of spices to your liking.

FOR 3 OR 4 PICKLES

Preparation time: 15 minutes
Cooking time: 5 minutes
Fermenting time: 5 days (minimum)
    to 4 weeks

BRINE INGREDIENTS

2 cups distilled water + as much
    as necessary for soaking
3 teaspoons coarse non-iodized salt

INGREDIENTS

9 oz pickling cucumbers
1 small bunch dill (with its flowers
    if possible)
2 bay leaves
1 garlic clove
3 teaspoons pickling spices
    (see note)

THE BRINE

In a saucepan, bring the distilled water and salt to a boil. When all the salt
is dissolved, remove from the heat and cool. This can be done in advance.

THE CUCUMBERS

Wash the cucumbers and remove the blossom ends (as opposed to the stem
ends). Unless your cucumbers have just been picked, soak them for 2 hours
in distilled water, which will make your finished pickles firmer.

THE JARS

Place the dill, bay leaves, garlic, and pickling spices in the bottom of a glass
or ceramic container that's just large enough to hold all the cucumbers
packed tightly together. After filling with the cucumbers, cover with the
cooled pickling brine to 4 inches above the top of the cucumbers. To keep
the cucumbers submerged, cover with a small plate weighted with a small
cup. Cover the jar with a clean dish towel, a piece of cheesecloth,
or an unsealed lid. Keep in a cool, dark place, outside of the refrigerator.

THE FERMENTATION

Every day or so, remove the scum that forms on the surface and, if necessary,
add a little more brine to keep the cucumbers submerged. After 4 or 5 days
at room temperature, the cucumbers will be partly fermented; they're what
we call "half sours." After 3 weeks, they will be completely fermented, or
"full sours." You then have your pickles. How long you ferment depends
on how sour you like your pickles. When they reach that point, you should
refrigerate your pickle container, which will drastically slow down the
fermentation process.

note: Pickling spices are made up of equal quantities, or any other combination,
of peppercorns, mustard seeds, coriander seeds, allspice, etc.

PUMPKIN MUFFINS

These pumpkin muffins taste like Christmas.
The little New York touch is the cream cheese in the middle.

MAKES 10 MUFFINS

Preparation time: 20 minutes
Cooking time: 20 minutes

DRY INGREDIENTS

2⅓ cups all-purpose flour
3 teaspoons baking powder
¾ cup light brown sugar
   (or ½ cup superfine sugar
   + 2 teaspoons molasses)
3 teaspoons ground cinnamon
1 teaspoon fine salt
1 teaspoon ground ginger
2 pinches ground nutmeg

WET INGREDIENTS

⅓ cup buttermilk
½ cup sunflower oil
2 eggs
1 teaspoon natural vanilla extract
15 oz can pumpkin purée
3¾ oz plain cream cheese
   (such as Philadelphia®)

THE BATTER

Preheat the oven to 425°F. Combine all the dry ingredients.
Whisk together the buttermilk, oil, eggs, and vanilla. Incorporate the
dry ingredients, mixing together quickly. Add the pumpkin purée, and
stir in without overworking the dough.

COOKING

Lightly grease 10 cups of a muffin pan, and fill each halfway with
the batter. Add 1 heaped teaspoon of cream cheese in the middle
of each cup and cover to the top with batter.
Bake the muffins for about 20 minutes until golden and a skewer
inserted near the middle comes out clean.

note: See pumpkin pie, page 184, for homemade pumpkin purée.

POP–TARTS®

This is a homemade version of one of my favorite snacks from when I was a child.

MAKES 9 SMALL POP-TARTS®

Preparation time: 40 minutes, plus cooling
Refrigeration time: 1 hour
Cooking time: 20 minutes

DOUGH

½ cup cold sweet/unsalted butter, diced
1⅔ cups all-purpose flour (or 1½ cups
    all-purpose flour + 3 teaspoons cocoa
    powder for the chocolate Pop-Tarts®)
½ teaspoon salt
1 oz confectioners' sugar
2½ tablespoons cold water
1½ teaspoons lemon juice

CHOCOLATE GANACHE

4 tablespoons half and half
2 tablespoons sweet/unsalted butter
4¼ oz chocolate, cut into pieces

BLUEBERRY FILLING

¼ cup blueberry jam (page 262)
3¾ oz whole blueberries

GLAZE

1 egg yolk
1 teaspoon water

FROSTING

1–2 tablespoons boiling water
1¾ cups confectioners' sugar
¼ cup raspberry jam (page 262)
chocolate sprinkles or other candy
    decorations, for sprinkling

THE DOUGH

Cut the butter into the dry ingredients (plain for the jam, or with cocoa for the chocolate Pop-Tarts®) using a food processor or knife. Next, incorporate the water and lemon juice by hand until you have a smooth dough. Roll into a ball, wrap in plastic wrap, and refrigerate for at least 1 hour.

THE CHOCOLATE GANACHE

In a saucepan, heat the cream and butter over medium heat until they come to a boil. Add the pieces of chocolate. Remove from the heat and let it melt for 1 minute. Stir with a spatula until smooth. The ganache is enough to fill nine Pop-Tarts®.

THE BLUEBERRY FILLING

Combine both the ingredients. The filling is enough to fill nine Pop-Tarts®.

SHAPING THE DOUGH

Preheat the oven to 350°F. On a floured work surface, roll out the dough into a rectangle about ⅛ inch thick, then cut into 18 small rectangles of the same size, and place half of them on a baking sheet lined with parchment paper.
Flatten the edges of the rectangles slightly with a floured finger, then place 3 teaspoons of filling in the middle of each, being careful to stay away from the edges. Moisten the edges of the rectangles with the filling using your finger, and top each one with another rectangle of dough. Avoiding pressing down on the filling in the middle, close the edges by pressing them lightly with a floured finger, and then seal them by pressing more firmly with a fork. Trim the excess dough and, using a sharp knife, make small incisions in the top.

COOKING

Combine the egg yolk and water and brush this mixture over the rectangles. Place in the oven and bake for about 20 minutes until they are well browned. Allow them to cool.

FROSTING

In a bowl, combine the water and sugar until smooth. Using a brush or spoon, spread this frosting on the Pop-Tarts®. Sprinkle over the decorations. For the raspberry frosting, heat the raspberry jam, strain it to remove the seeds, and use instead of the hot water in the plain frosting.

BANANA STICKS

Kids love making and eating these, as do I!

MAKES 8 STICKS

Preparation time: 10 minutes
Cooking time: 5 minutes
Freezing time: 5 hours

INGREDIENTS

4 bananas
1 cup dark/semisweet chocolate,
    chopped
2 teaspoons coconut oil or butter
1½ tablespoons boiling water
    (or more if necessary)
2 teaspoons sugar syrup (page 176)
chopped nuts or colored sprinkles,
    for decorating

THE STICKS

Cut the bananas in half and insert popsicle sticks into the flat ends. Individually wrap the half bananas in plastic wrap and place them in the freezer for at least 5 hours ahead of time.

THE SAUCE

Melt the chocolate with the oil or butter over low heat in a double boiler. Mix in the boiling water and sugar syrup. If the chocolate starts to thicken too much from sitting, add a little hot water.

ASSEMBLY

Holding a frozen banana by the stick, dip it into the chocolate mixture. Using a pastry brush, brush the chocolate up the sides of the banana and over the bottom, so that it is completely covered. Lift the banana out of the pan and gently tilt and turn it to allow any excess chocolate to drip off. Immediately sprinkle it with any extra toppings of your choice (chopped peanuts, for example) before the chocolate sets, and place it on a baking sheet lined with parchment paper.

SERVING

Serve immediately, or return to the freezer. If refreezing, you might want to let the banana sticks warm up for a couple of minutes out of the freezer before serving as they can be quite hard when they first come out.

note: Popsicle sticks are available online or in some specialty food and craft stores. Just make sure they are labeled "food grade." You can also reuse the sticks from store-bought ice creams, or replace the popsicle sticks with something else, like an upside-down disposable teaspoon or a coffee stirrer.

CHOCOLATE PEANUT BUTTER CUPS

Here's an incredibly easy homemade rendition of the famous Reese's Peanut Butter Cups®.

MAKES 15 MINI MOUTHFULS

Preparation time: 10 minutes
Cooking time: 5 minutes
Freezing time: 10 minutes

INGREDIENTS

1 tablespoon coconut oil
10 oz dark/semisweet chocolate,
   chopped
5½ oz crunchy peanut butter
   (page 263)

THE CHOCOLATE

In a saucepan, melt the coconut oil and chocolate together over low heat. Mix with a spatula until smooth.

Stack several small paper baking cups inside each other: It helps keep the paper pleat intact, otherwise the pressure of the chocolate pushes out the sides and distorts the shape.

Using a ratio of two parts chocolate to one part peanut butter, pour a little of the chocolate–oil mixture into the bottom of a paper baking cup and allow the mixture to set in the refrigerator for a few minutes.

ASSEMBLY

Add a little peanut butter into the middle of each cup, then cover with more of the chocolate–oil mixture. Repeat the process with the other baking cups and place everything in the freezer for at least 10 minutes.

SERVING

Once the peanut butter cups have frozen solid, you can remove the extra reinforcing layers of paper baking cups.

Take the cups out of the freezer a minute or so before serving.

MACADAMIA NUT COOKIES

Macadamia nuts and white chocolate—a win-win combination.

MAKES 20 COOKIES

Preparation time: 20 minutes, plus cooling
Refrigeration time: 1 hour
Cooking time: 9 minutes

INGREDIENTS

1 cup sweet/unsalted butter, softened
1¼ cups superfine sugar
2⅓ cups all-purpose flour
1¾ oz baby oat flakes or quick oats
½ teaspoon baking powder
½ teaspoon salt
2 eggs
1 teaspoon natural vanilla extract
4½ oz white chocolate, chopped
   (or 4½ oz white chocolate chips)
4½ oz macadamia nuts, chopped

THE DOUGH

Using an electric mixer, beat the butter and sugar vigorously until light and creamy. Mix together the flour, oats, baking powder, and salt. In a bowl, whisk the eggs with the vanilla.

Incorporate the dry ingredients into the butter–sugar mixture alternately with the eggs, mixing well after each addition. Finally, add the pieces of white chocolate and the macadamia nuts. Mix again. Shape into a ball, wrap loosely in plastic wrap and refrigerate for at least 1 hour.

CUTTING AND COOKING

Preheat the oven to 400°F. Divide the dough into 20 balls, place them on two baking sheets lined with parchment paper, leaving about 1¼ inches between each, and bake them for about 9 minutes. The cookies should still be quite soft when they come out of the oven. Allow them to cool for at least 10 minutes at room temperature before serving.

ICED COFFEE

See recipe page 12.

BLUE
CUP

This recipe is a twist on the traditional acai cup, using blueberries instead of acai berries.

SERVES 4
Preparation time: 5 minutes

INGREDIENTS
10½ oz frozen banana
10½ oz frozen blueberries
4¼ oz avocado
1½ tablespoons maple syrup, honey,
   or agave syrup (optional)
¼ cup water

THE MIX
Blend all the ingredients together in a food processor or blender. If the frozen fruit is too hard, let it thaw for a few minutes before blending. If you don't have a food processor, you could mash everything up with a fork for a chunkier version.
Serve like a frozen yogurt with toppings, such as fresh fruit and granola.

GRANOLA
See recipe page 54.

note: The acai is a Brazilian palm tree whose fruit, acai berries, have a high concentration of blue pigment, a very powerful antioxidant. Unfortunately, acai berries can be a little expensive and difficult to find. I prefer blueberries, which are not only loaded with blue antioxidant pigment but are also easier to source. I happen to think they taste better, too. That said, you can certainly replace the frozen blueberries with frozen acai berries if you find them.

MINI MUFFINS

These little bombshells rework mixtures used in other recipes.

MAKES 30 MINI CHEESECAKES

Preparation time: 25 minutes, plus cooling
Cooking time: 10 minutes
Refrigeration time: 1 hour

INGREDIENTS

1 quantity homemade Oreo® dough
   (page 230)
7½ oz plain cream cheese
   (such as Philadelphia®)
¼ cup superfine sugar
1 pinch salt
3 teaspoons all-purpose flour
½ lemon, juice and finely shredded zest
7 oz sour cream
2 eggs
3 drops natural vanilla extract

MAKES 18 MINI BROWNIES

Preparation time: 25 minutes, plus cooling
Cooking time: 25 minutes

INGREDIENTS

1 quantity brownie dough (page 222)
1 large banana, not too ripe
¼ cup peanuts, coarsely chopped
1 teaspoon fine sea salt

MINI CHEESECAKES

THE OREO® DOUGH AND CREAM CHEESE

Make the Oreo® dough and cheesecake mixture following the instructions on pages 230 and 196.

SHAPING AND COOKING

Preheat the oven to 425°F. Divide the Oreo® dough into 20 small balls. Place 20 thick paper or foil baking cups, 20 silicon molds approximately 2½ inches in diameter and 1½ inches high, or two greased and floured muffin pans, on a baking sheet. Place a ball of dough in each mold, and spread it over the bottom and side with your fingers, without going to the top of the mold. Pour the cream cheese filling on top of the Oreo® dough, filling the molds to the top. Bake for about 10 minutes. Allow to cool completely before eating.

MINI BROWNIES

THE BROWNIE DOUGH

Make the brownie dough by following the instructions on page 222.

ASSEMBLY AND COOKING

Preheat the oven to 350°F.
Butter and flour 12 individual silicon molds approximately 2½ inches in diameter and 1½ inches high. Fill the molds with the batter to the top. With a wet hand, flatten, and smooth the surface. Cut the banana into slices ¼ inch thick, and insert a round into the batter in the middle of each muffin. Sprinkle the top of the mini muffins with the crushed peanuts, then the fine sea salt.
Bake for about 20 minutes; the top of the mini muffins becomes solid to the touch and the inside is melting. Allow to cool for at least 30 minutes before serving.

00:00

EXTRAS

THE BASIC RECIPES

STRAWBERRY JAM

*My colleague, Eugénie, makes her strawberry jam
the old-fashioned way, with no added pectin.*

MAKES 2 LB 12 OZ
Preparation time: 20 minutes
Cooking time: 20–25 minutes
Resting time: 12 hours

INGREDIENTS
2 lb 4 oz strawberries
3¼ cups granulated sugar
3 tablespoons lemon juice
vanilla bean, halved lengthways

THE DAY BEFORE
Rinse, dry, and hull the strawberries, then cut them in half or quarters,
depending on their size. Put them in a bowl, add the remaining ingredients,
and combine well. Cover and refrigerate overnight.

PREPARATION
To check whether your jam is ready without a sugar thermometer, you
can use the cold saucer test. In this case, place three small clean saucers
in the freezer at least 30 minutes before you start cooking the jam.

COOKING
Take the macerated strawberries out of the refrigerator and pour into
a jam pan or a large stainless steel saucepan. Bring to a boil over high
heat. The mixture will start to froth up.
Stir the mixture regularly and make sure it doesn't overflow the pan.
Carefully remove any scum that forms on top using a skimmer or
a tablespoon. Lower the heat and continue cooking over medium
heat for 20–25 minutes.

THE RIGHT TEMPERATURE
Turn off the heat and place a sugar thermometer in the pan, making sure
it doesn't touch the bottom or the sides. The jam is ready when it reaches
220°F. Otherwise, return to the heat until it reaches the right temperature.
Without a sugar thermometer, check the setting point of the jam by dipping
in a tablespoon and lifting it above the pan. If the mixture runs off in a thin
stream, the jam is not ready. However, if it forms drops as it starts to flow,
take out one of the small plates from the freezer and pour 1 teaspoon of jam
onto it: The jam is ready when it sets on contact with the cold plate.
Otherwise, return to the heat for a few minutes before repeating the test.

STORING
Remove the vanilla bean, and pour the jam into clean jars. It can be stored
in the refrigerator for 3–4 weeks. Sterilize the jars for a longer shelf life.

RASPBERRY JAM

*In this raspberry jam of Eugénie's, the scent and
taste of lime goes very well with the raspberries,
but feel free to replace it with lemon.*

MAKES 2 LB 12 OZ
Preparation time: 20 minutes
Cooking time: about 15 minutes

INGREDIENTS
2 lb 4 oz fresh raspberries
3¼ cups granulated sugar
zest of 1 lime
2 tablespoons lime (or lemon) juice

Place the raspberries, sugar, lime zest, and juice in a jam pan or a stainless
steel saucepan and heat over high heat. Proceed as for the strawberry jam.
Since raspberries are higher in pectin than strawberries, the cooking time
will be shorter and the jam will set more quickly.

*tip: If you make your raspberry jam this way, you get a jam with a lot of seeds,
which some people may not like. You can put all or some of the raspberries through
a food mill to remove the seeds before you start cooking the jam.*

BLUEBERRY JAM

This is Eugénie's recipe without added pectin.

MAKES 2 LB 12 OZ
Preparation time: 20 minutes
Cooking time: about 15 minutes
Resting time: 12 hours

INGREDIENTS
2 lb 4 oz blueberries (wild blueberries if possible)
3¼ cups granulated sugar
5 tablespoons lemon juice (approximately the juice of 1 lemon)
zest of 1 lemon

The day before, pick over the blueberries and rinse them very quickly under
cold water. Place them in a jam pan or a large stainless steel saucepan and
heat to a simmer. Turn off the heat, pour into a large heatproof bowl
and allow to cool. Cover the mixture with plastic wrap, placing the wrap
in contact with the surface of the fruit, and refrigerate overnight.
The next day, return the mixture to the pan, add the sugar, and lemon juice
and zest, and cook over high heat for about 15 minutes, checking the
mixture regularly with the cold plate test (see "strawberry jam") or a sugar
thermometer. It should indicate 220°F. Pour the jam into clean jars and store
in the refrigerator. Sterilize the jars for a longer shelf life.

APPLE JELLY

MAKES ABOUT 2 CUPS

Preparation time: 20 minutes
Cooking time: 55 minutes
Resting time: 8–12 hours

INGREDIENTS

2 lb 12 oz granny smith apples (or other cooking apples)
3¼ cups water (for an estimated yield of 3¼ cups juice)
1½ tablespoons lemon juice
2¼ cups sugar
¼ vanilla bean
2 teaspoons butter

THE APPLE JUICE

Roughly chop the apples, including the skin and seeds, and simmer in water for 15–20 minutes. Place the apples in a store-bought jelly bag, or a homemade equivalent, then let the juice drip and filter through without pressing for 8–12 hours (ideally overnight). Measure the filtered juice and adjust the amount of lemon juice and sugar proportionally. For example, for 1¾ cups juice, you will need 2 teaspoons lemon juice, 1 cup of sugar, and so on.

PREPARATION

To check whether the jam is ready without a sugar thermometer, use the cold saucer test: Place three small clean saucers in the freezer at least 30 minutes before you start cooking the jam.

COOKING

Combine the filtered juice with the lemon juice and sugar in a saucepan. Stir constantly over low heat. Once the sugar has dissolved, bring the mixture to a low boil, continuing to stir. Place the sugar thermometer into the mixture at this point, still stirring, until the mixture reaches 220°F. Turn off the heat and let the jelly stand for 5 minutes, then turn the heat back on to bring the jelly back to 220°F.

THE RIGHT CONSISTENCY

Instead of, or as well as the thermometer method, you can test whether the jelly is ready by spooning 1 teaspoon jelly on one of the plates chilled in advance in the freezer. Start doing this test after about 5 minutes of boiling. The jelly is ready when the mixture sets on contact with the cold plate. If this doesn't happen, repeat the test every 5 minutes until you get the desired result, turning the heat off while you perform the test.

STORING

Mix in the butter and vanilla and transfer the jelly to clean jars. Allow to cool and store in the refrigerator.

GRAPE JELLY

MAKES ABOUT 2 CUPS

Preparation time: 20 minutes
Cooking time: 50 minutes
Resting time: 10–15 hours

INGREDIENTS

1 lb 9 oz granny smith apples
1⅓ cups water, boiling (for an estimated yield of 2¾ cups juice)
1 lb 7 oz muscat grapes
6 tablespoons lemon juice
2¾ cups sugar

THE JUICE

Roughly chop the apples, including the skin and seeds, and simmer in the boiling water for about 5 minutes. Crush the grapes between your hands or with a potato masher, add them to the apples and water, and simmer for another 5 minutes. Cover the saucepan, turn off the heat and let the mixture stand for 2–3 hours.

THE JELLY

Pass the mixture through a medium-hole strainer and allow the mixture to drip through a jelly bag, or its homemade equivalent, for 8–12 hours, as for the apple jelly. Measure the filtered juice and adjust the amount of each of the other ingredients accordingly, based on the proportions given above for 2¾ cups. Cook and store as described in the recipe for apple jelly.

tip: Don't throw away the fruit pulp left in the jelly bag, sieve it to make an excellent apple (or apple and grape) sauce, which you can sweeten or flavor to taste. The flavor of the apple and grape sauce reminds me of lychees.

WHIPPED CREAM

SERVES 8

Preparation time: 15 minutes

INGREDIENTS

1 cup heavy/whipping cream
2½ tablespoons confectioners' sugar
1 teaspoon natural vanilla extract

At least 15 minutes before you begin, place the bowl and whisk in the refrigerator along with the cream. Begin whipping the cream with an electric mixer on a low speed. Increase the speed gradually while adding the sugar through a sifter to avoid lumps. Add the vanilla and continue whipping until the cream is firm.

PEANUT BUTTER

Here's a simple way to make peanut butter at home without a special grinder.

MAKES ABOUT 1 LB 5 OZ

Preparation time: 5 minutes

INGREDIENTS

1 lb 2 oz peanuts, roasted and salted
1½ oz coconut oil
1½ tablespoons peanut oil (for smoothness)
1½ tablespoons light honey

Blend all the ingredients together in a food processor until smooth. Add more oil if necessary for the desired smoothness.

KETCHUP

This is my basic recipe. You can experiment with a few twists: Replace the white vinegar with balsamic vinegar, and add some cayenne or red chili pepper with the onions and celery …

MAKES 2¼ CUPS
Preparation time: 15 minutes
Cooking time: 23 minutes

STOCK
1 tablespoon finely chopped celery
1 tablespoon finely chopped onion
1 teaspoon olive oil
1⅓ cups water

OTHER INGREDIENTS
5 oz concentrated tomato purée
⅓ cup superfine sugar
2 pinches salt
small pinch ground nutmeg
1 tablespoon cornstarch
3 tablespoons white vinegar

THE STOCK
Sauté the celery and onion in the oil for 3 minutes, then add the water and bring to a boil. Lower the heat and simmer for 10 minutes. Strain, reserving the liquid. You need 1⅓ cups liquid, so add water to make up volume, if needed.

THE KETCHUP
Combine the strained liquid, concentrated tomato purée, sugar, salt, and nutmeg in a saucepan. Bring to a boil over medium heat, then lower the heat and simmer for 5 minutes, stirring. Blend the cornstarch with the vinegar. Pour this mixture into the saucepan and simmer for another 5 minutes, stirring.

SERVING
Allow to cool before serving. Store in the refrigerator in a bottle.

DELI MUSTARD

Here is a simple recipe for a basic deli mustard that would be perfect for hot dogs or knishes.

MAKES ABOUT 2 CUPS
Preparation time: 15 minutes
Resting time: 1 day

INGREDIENTS
½ cup yellow mustard seeds
2 pinches salt
3 teaspoons dried turmeric
2 tablespoons all-purpose flour
2 tablespoons light honey or sugar
1¼ cups cider vinegar

Grind the mustard seeds into a fine powder in a coffee or spice grinder (or use about 3 oz/85 grams mustard powder). Combine with the salt, turmeric, and flour. Mix the honey and vinegar together. Combine with the dry mixture, using a fork, until smooth. If it seems a little thin, this is normal since the mustard will thicken on standing. Cover and leave out for a day at room temperature for the flavors to mingle a little. Store in the refrigerator.

MAYONNAISE

Make your own mayonnaise. It's easy to do and, more importantly, it will be better than the bought version for a couple of reasons: It will be fresh and you will decide what goes into it. Here's the basic recipe I use.

MAKES ABOUT 1 CUP
Preparation time: 15 minutes

INGREDIENTS
1 egg yolk
1 pinch salt
1 teaspoon sugar
1 teaspoon white vinegar or lemon juice
⅔ cup sunflower or canola oil

VARIATIONS
add 1 or both of the following ingredients:
1 teaspoon Dijon mustard
1–3 garlic cloves, crushed

PREPARATION
All the ingredients should be at room temperature to facilitate the emulsion. So if you keep your eggs in the refrigerator, take them out at least 30 minutes ahead of time. If you add garlic, crush it as finely as possible, ideally into a paste using a mortar and pestle.

THE MAYONNAISE
In a deep bowl, whisk everything, except the oil, until combined. Continue whisking while dripping in the oil very slowly. As the mayonnaise starts to thicken, you can add the oil more quickly, but if you add the oil too quickly at the start, the emulsion may not take, (i.e. the ingredients may separate).

CROUTONS

Croutons are an important element in many soups and salads and, in some cases, such as split pea soup or Caesar salad, I consider them to be an integral part of the recipe.

MAKES ABOUT 1 LB
Preparation time: 10 minutes
Cooking time: about 10 minutes

INGREDIENTS
1 lb stale bread, cut into equal cubes
¼ cup olive oil
3 tablespoons melted butter or your choice of oil
1–2 pinches salt
1 teaspoon dried herbs
½ teaspoon garlic powder (optional)

Preheat the oven to 450°F. In a bowl, mix together the cubes of stale bread with the other ingredients. Spread them out on a baking tray and bake for about 10 minutes until they are golden brown.
You can also cook them in a frying pan. This is a good method if you want to make small batches, say for 3–4 servings of salad. In this case, after mixing the ingredients, fry the croutons over medium heat, tossing and stirring them for 5–10 minutes until they are evenly browned.

tip: If you use fresh bread, dry it out a little by putting the cubes in a preheated 200°F oven for about 10 minutes.

HOME FRIES

Here is a basic technique to make fries in the oven.

FOR 2 LB 4 OZ VEGETABLES
Preparation time: 10 minutes
Cooking time: 30–45 minutes

INGREDIENTS
2 lb 4 oz root vegetables; allow about 3½–7 oz per serving
   (while pale-skinned potatoes are most common, red-skinned potatoes,
   sweet potatoes, parsnips, or beets are fantastic alternatives)
salt and spices
cooking oil

CUTTING
Preheat the oven to 450°F. Line a baking tray with parchment paper. Peel
and clean the selected root vegetables and cut into small uniform pieces.

FLAVORINGS
Place the chopped vegetables in a large bowl and toss in a little salt and
spices (such as ground pepper, herbes de Provence, cumin, etc.) and
combine. Which spices and how much you add is up to you, but it's better
to err on the side of too little, since you can always add more salt, pepper,
and condiments to taste at the table.

COOKING
Generously drizzle the vegetables with cooking oil and mix by hand to coat,
adding more oil as needed. Spread the oiled vegetables on the baking tray
in one layer and bake for 30–45 minutes, taking the vegetables out of the
oven about every 15 minutes to turn them and ultimately to check whether
they're cooked.

COLESLAW

*It's hard to imagine having a burger, or any sort of sandwich
for that matter, without a side of this classic cabbage salad.*

MAKES 20 SMALL SERVINGS
Preparation time: 10 minutes
Resting time: 12–24 hours

INGREDIENTS
1 lb 4 oz cabbage, cored, and outer leaves removed
3½ oz carrot

DRESSING
3 tablespoons sugar
1½ tablespoons white wine vinegar flavored with tarragon
¼ cup mayonnaise (page 264)
2¼ oz yogurt
2 pinches salt and ½ pinch pepper

THE CABBAGE AND CARROTS
Shred the cabbage and carrot using a food processor, a knife, or a handheld
shredder. I like it to be shredded as finely as possible. Whatever method you
use, shred the cabbage and carrot to the same size.

THE DRESSING
Combine the dressing ingredients and mix with the cabbage and carrot.
The dressing will at first be quite thick, then it will thin out as the vegetables
release their juices. Let the coleslaw marinate for 12–24 hours in the
refrigerator before serving.

ONION RINGS

Onion rings are just that little bit more special than french fries.

SERVES 2
Preparation time: 10 minutes
Cooking time: 3 minutes per batch

INGREDIENTS
2 large onions, oil for frying

BATTER: WET INGREDIENTS
½ cup milk
1 egg

BATTER: DRY INGREDIENTS
½ cup all-purpose flour
2 tablespoons cornstarch
3 pinches baking powder, 3 pinches sugar
1 pinch salt, 1 pinch paprika

THE BATTER
In a deep-fryer or large saucepan, heat some oil until it reaches 350°F.
Make the batter by mixing the wet and dry ingredients together separately.
Whisk the two mixtures together until smooth.

THE ONIONS
Peel and cut the onions into slices ½–¾ inch thick and separate into rings.

FRYING
Dip the onion rings into the batter, allowing the excess to drain off, and fry
for about 3 minutes until golden brown, turning them over halfway through.
Start frying by testing the oil with a small ring of onion. If it cooks too slowly
or too quickly, adjust the oil temperature. Make sure you allow the oil to heat
back up for a few minutes between batches.

SERVING
Drain the onion rings on some paper towels. Keep them in an oven preheated
to 200°F if not serving immediately. Season with salt.

CHICKEN STOCK

*Transform your chicken carcass into precious stock,
a base ingredient in any number of soups and sauces.*

MAKES ABOUT 8 CUPS
Preparation time: 10 minutes
Cooking time: 3 hours

INGREDIENTS
9 oz cooked chicken carcass (skin and meat removed)
12 cups cold water
5½ oz onion, 1¾ oz carrot, 1¾ oz celery
1 bunch parsley, 2 bay leaves
2 teaspoons salt and 1 teaspoon peppercorns

Combine all the ingredients in a large pot. Bring to a boil, then lower heat to
minimum and cook for at least 3 hours, uncovered, skimming off any scum
that forms on the surface about every 30 minutes. Cool the stock and strain to
remove all solids. There should be about 8 cups of stock, which, if not used
immediately, can be stored for several days in the refrigerator or frozen.

note: *A lot of cooks reduce their stock by half or more before freezing. Concentrated
stock can be made into ice cubes and extended with water when used in recipes.*

RECIPE INDEX

INGREDIENT INDEX

ADDRESSES

MANHATTAN

BROADWAY RESTAURANT
2664 BROADWAY
NEW YORK, NY 10025

A friendly, no-frills Greek diner, with great eggs, a very good meatloaf and gravy, burgers, and other sandwiches. The BLT is made with a religious perfection.

DOUGHNUT PLANT
379 GRAND STREET
NEW YORK, NY 10002

Simply the best doughnuts in New York. The crème brûlée is a marvel.

EISENBERG'S SANDWICH SHOP
174 5TH AVENUE
NEW YORK, NY 10010

This quaint diner is my food-loving brother's favorite when he wants a classic coffee shop meal like a tuna melt sandwich or a matzo ball soup.

HOP SHING RESTAURANT
9 CHATHAM SQUARE
NEW YORK, NY 10038

The authenticity of this Chinese coffee shop is undeniable. Treat yourself to an egg custard pie or a pork bun with a cup of piping-hot filter coffee. You will not be disappointed.

KATZ'S DELICATESSEN
205 EAST HOUSTON STREET
NEW YORK, NY 10002

The oldest delicatessen in New York. They still come up with the goods. I recommend the Katz's Corned Beef. Believe me, it's not for nothing they sell more than 2 tons a week.

KOSSAR'S BIALYS
367 GRAND STREET
NEW YORK, NY 10002

This kosher bakery makes the best bialys in New York.

MELVIN'S JUICE BOX
130 WEST HOUSTON STREET
NEW YORK, NY 10012

The warm presence of Melvin and his inspired blends make this my favorite juice bar in Manhattan. I particularly like the PB&J smoothie.

MURRAY'S BAGELS
500 AVENUE OF THE AMERICAS
NEW YORK, NY 10011

Here, the bagels are made the old-fashioned way: Hand-rolled and slowly fermented. My favorite: The cinnamon–raisin.

MURRAY'S STURGEON SHOP
2429 BROADWAY
NEW YORK, NY 10024

This tiny Jewish deli is a temple for old continental delicacies: Smoked fish, pickled meats, noodle kugel, strudel, rugelach…And you will not find a better smoked salmon bagel anywhere.

PHO PASTEUR RESTAURANT
85 BAXTER STREET
NEW YORK, NY 10013

I've been going to this Vietnamese restaurant (one of the first to open in Chinatown) for years. My pet dishes: Caramelized claypot fish and green papaya salad.

RUSS & DAUGHTERS
179 EAST HOUSTON STREET
NEW YORK, NY 10002

This small family deli is an institution for all the dishes from the old continent like smoked salmon, pickled herring, and caviar. I expect to take my grandchildren there one day.

SECOND AVENUE DELI
162 EAST 33RD STREET
NEW YORK, NY 10016

They say the pastrami sandwiches from this traditional kosher delicatessen are the best in town. They also make a notable matzo ball soup.

STAGE RESTAURANT
128 2ND AVENUE
NEW YORK, NY 10003

I love this Ukrainian greasy spoon for its Eastern European classics: Pierogi, latkes, borscht.

THE PICKLE GUYS
49 ESSEX STREET
NEW YORK, NY 10002

For slowly marinated old-style pickles, there's no place better. Everything from classic Kirby cucumbers to spiced pineapple.

TOM'S RESTAURANT
2880 BROADWAY
NEW YORK, NY 10025

This iconic Greek diner gained its fame from "Seinfeld", but above all it's been the favorite restaurant of Columbia University students for over 70 years.

YONAH SCHIMMEL KNISH BAKERY
137 EAST HOUSTON STREET
NEW YORK, NY 10002

This bakery only does one thing but does it well: Knishes.

BROOKLYN

BAKERI
150 WYTHE AVENUE
BROOKLYN, NY 11211

A super-cute café with divine cookies and cakes, all served with excellent coffee. The waitresses in their Norwegian mechanic's overalls also add to the charm of the place.

CAFÉ DE LA ESQUINA
225 WYTHE AVENUE
BROOKLYN, NY 11211

This is the former Wythe Diner, converted into a Mexican restaurant. The atmosphere has stayed intact. This is the perfect place to enjoy tacos, tortilla soup, and huevos rancheros, or sip on a spicy lemonade.

FOUR & TWENTY BLACKBIRDS
439 3RD AVENUE
BROOKLYN, NY 11215

If pies were a religion, this café–bakery in the hip Gowanus Canal neighborhood in Brooklyn would be its temple. The honey pie is a revelation!

JUNIOR'S
386 FLATBUSH AVE EXT
BROOKLYN, NY 11201

This enormous coffee shop-style restaurant is the benchmark for New York cheesecake. Its reputation is deserved.

MARLOW & DAUGHTERS
95 BROADWAY
BROOKLYN, NY 11211

With its neighbors Marlow & Sons and Diner, this butcher with old-fashioned charm is part of the hipster back-to-basics movement that has developed in Williamsburg in recent years.

PETER PAN DONUT & PASTRY
727 MANHATTAN AVENUE
BROOKLYN, 11211

This old-style Polish doughnut shop in Greenpoint is the perfect place to enjoy the classics: Honey-glazed doughnuts, jam, or chocolate doughnuts, or the Boston cream.

SMORGASBURG (MARKET)
27 NORTH 6TH STREET
BROOKLYN, NY 11211

On Saturdays, on the bank of the East River opposite Manhattan, this incredible market comes alive, bringing together local artisan producers come to show off their products: Craft beer, pickles, snow cones, grilled cheeseburgers, and s'mores.

ACKNOWLEDGEMENTS

BEHIND THE SCENES

Rose-Marie Di Domenico – editor
Pauline Labrousse – editor
Eugénie Lopez Ioualalen – head chef
Cécile Mayot – graphic design
Moa Dahlgren – recipe illustrator
Emilie Collet – food preparation

COOKS

Jean-Pierre Ahtuam
Sara Jane Crawford
Dorottya Czegledi
Eugénie Lopez Ioualalen
Gavin Smart
Ngan Tran
Amaury De Veyrac

BIG THANKS

Steven Alan
Sandrine Cooper
Arlette Coron
Gabriel Coron
Élisabeth Darets-Chochod
Paul Feldsher
Jerry Grant
Roslyn Grant
Anne Shapiro-Niel
Emmanuel Le Vallois
Magali Veillon
Ayla Yavin

STERLING EPICURE
New York

An Imprint of Sterling Publishing
387 Park Avenue South
New York, NY 10016

This edition published in 2014 by Sterling Publishing Co., Inc.
First published in France in 2012 by Marabout. Published in Australia in 2013 by Murdoch Books.

Design by Hachette Livre (Marabout)
Styling by Sabrina Fauda-Rôle
Art Direction by Fabienne Coron
Translation by Melissa McMahon

ISBN 978-1-4549-1206-4

Distributed in Canada by Sterling Publishing
c/o Canadian Manda Group, 165 Dufferin Street
Toronto, Ontario, Canada M6K 3H6

For information about custom editions, special sales, and premium and corporate purchases, please
contact Sterling Special Sales at 800-805-5489 or specialsales@sterlingpublishing.com.

Manufactured in China

10 9 8 7 6 5 4 3 2 1

www.sterlingpublishing.com

IMPORTANT: Those who might be at risk from the effects of salmonella poisoning (the elderly, pregnant women, young children,
and those suffering from immune deficiency diseases) should consult their doctor with any concerns about eating raw eggs.

OVEN GUIDE: You may find cooking times vary depending on the oven you are using. For fan-forced ovens,
as a general rule, set the oven temperature to 35°F (20°C) lower than indicated in the recipe.

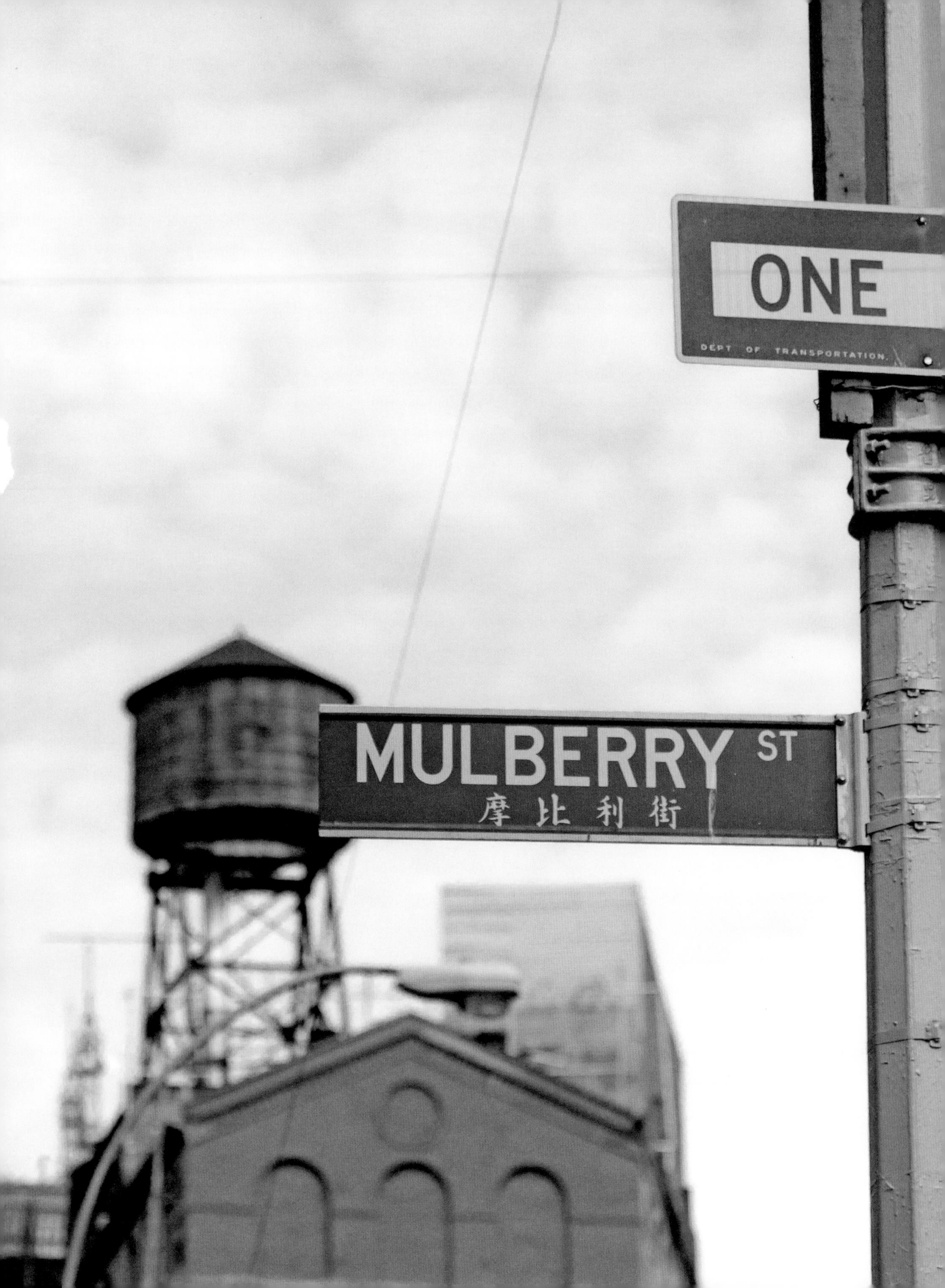
ONE
DEPT OF TRANSPORTATION
MULBERRY ST
摩比利街

MURRAY'S BAGEL'S
500 AVENUE OF THE AMERICAS
MANHATTAN

MELVIN'S JUICE BOX
130 WEST HOUSTON STREET
MANHATTAN

KATZ'S DELICATESSEN
205 EAST HOUSTON STREET
MANHATTAN

HOP SHING RESTAURANT
9 CHATHAM SQUARE
MANHATTAN

EISENBURG'S SANDWICH SHOP
174 5TH AVENUE
MANHATTAN

DOUGHNUT PLANT
379 GRAND STREET
MANHATTAN

THE PICKLE GUYS
49 ESSEX STREET
MANHATTAN

STAGE RESTAURANT
128 2ND AVENUE
MANHATTAN

SMORGASBURG
27 NORTH 6TH STREET
BROOKLYN

RUSS AND DAUGHTERS
179 EAST HOUSTON STREET
MANHATTAN

YONAH SCHIMMEL'S KNISH BAKERY
137 EAST HOUSTON STREET
MANHATTAN

2ND AVENUE DELI
162 EAST 33RD STREET
MANHATTAN

PHO PASTEUR RESTAURANT
85 BAXTER STREET
MANHATTAN

4 AND 20 BLACKBIRDS
439 3RD AVENUE
BROOKLYN

PETER PAN DONUT AND PASTRY
727 MANHATTAN AVENUE
BROOKLYN

MARLOW AND DAUGHTERS
95 BROADWAY
BROOKLYN

BAKERI
150 WYTHE AVENUE
BROOKLYN

CAFE DE LA ESQUINA
225 WYTHE AVENUE
BROOKLYN